OCCUPY
Consciousness

Peter McGugan

Potentials Press Canada

www.ConsciousWorldSummit.com

Published in 2012 by Potentials Press Canada

LIBRARY OF CONGRESS CATALOGUE-IN-PUBLICATION DATA

Occupy Consciousness
by McGUGAN, PETER

Includes Index
ISBN 978-0-9694312-4-4

1. Self Help   2. Business

cover design by
Peter McGugan and Bob Deck

Acknowledgments

The author and publisher are very grateful for the generosity of the following people:

Wayne Forrest Reel
Emily Andrews
John Boswell
Diana von Welanetz Wentworth
Mary E. D'Aprix
Mary Olsen Kelly

Table of Contents

Prologue

We've been taught to capitalize the names of things our culture considers valuable or significant.

We capitalize people's names.

We capitalize street names, the names of villages and towns, counties, states and countries—i.e., we capitalize real estate.

We capitalize the names of manmade institutions and companies because we capitalize what moves money.

Capitalization is a society's way of saying, "Attention! This matters!"

During the agricultural, industrial and information ages we did not capitalize "earth," "universe," "galaxy," or "cosmos," considering them not real or important.

Think about it.

We've been thoroughly conditioned to think very small, taught to keep closed minds that will contain only small, obedient thoughts.

As a consequence, we've dropped down out of higher Consciousness and the wisdom, peace and instincts it delivers.

Because they are very real and vitally important, I do capitalize "Earth," "Universe," "Galaxy," "Cosmos," and sometimes big realities such as "Consciousness", "Creation", "Presence", "Life" and "BEing."

It jolts our awareness of what really matters.

We've placed Life in peril as 50,000 species a year, throughout the food chain, go extinct and our Mother Earth develops pneumonia.

The change, the shift you're feeling, is Life saving Life and that's what this book and consciousworldsummit.com are supporting.

Introduction

I Love that everything is atoms and molecules dancing with a third presence that Loves to create Life on Earth. I Love Loving Life.

Creation Consciousness is the name I'm using to identify Life's orchestrating Presence.

If you label the architect of Life, the Lord, God Almighty, the Creator, the Maker, Allah, Jehovah, Yahweh, the Father, the Son, the Holy Ghost, Holy Spirit, the Holy Trinity, the Great Spirit, Gitchi Manitou, the Tao, a fluke, or any of hundreds of other languaged and religiously branded names, it's all describing the ongoing happening of Creation flowing through everything.

Names are simply cultural arrows pointing in the direction of an energy. A name is just one language's label—it's the truth of an energy presence that matters.

This is why a dog is often a better judge of character than the people who read pedigrees.

Medicine confuses cognizance with Consciousness. If someone passes out, we say they've "lost consciousness". But they haven't. They've lost cognizance—awareness.

Consciousness is an orchestrating, architectural energy realm not susceptible to polarity.

The brighter and more open your Consciousness is, the higher the quality of awareness, health, wisdom and experience you're having. High Consciousness enlightens and lifts us individually and then socially.

Low consciousness drops us down into the fear, greed, collapse and chaos stratas of destructive energy.

The Spectrum of Consciousness

Just as sound and light can be focused with high vibrational spectrums, Consciousness can be centered and vibrationally high, or shattered, dark and low.

As high Consciousness we're enlightened and creatively expansive. Ease, creativity, community and grace flow at the high vibrations.

Crisis and cruelty can shatter Consciousness, turning people into insatiably addictive, energy sucking, destructive black holes.

Every crisis humanity struggles with is the crisis of low consciousness.

This book explores how higher Consciousness creates Life and prosperity and low consciousness creates chaos and misery.

For many centuries aristocracies have deliberately unplugged humanity from being higher Consciousness, and the days of reckoning are upon us all.

Extreme Confusion

We're living a temporary, low consciousness age of extremes.

Extremes are unsustainable because they're positioned out at the deviant ends of possibility.

Extremities fray. Balance is centered.

We're all witnessing social and economic collapse, income inequality, climate crisis, senseless war and an obscenely powerful and pervasive Illuminati elite that's warlording over the global population.

We're in societies that dress rascals in robes and integrity in rags.

In a 2011 speech, broadcaster Bill Moyers said, "Our politicians are little more than money launderers in the trafficking of power and policy— fewer than six degrees of separation from the spirit and tactics of Tony Soprano."

There's an ongoing collapse of health care, education, justice, government effectiveness, media integrity, quality of food, weather, health and overall quality of life.

The poorest 60% of Americans now have a measly 4.3% of the wealth.

The richest 20% have 84% of the wealth, and they're hoarding, retiring or investing overseas.

If you want the story in a compelling narrative, read *Winner-Take-All Politics: How Washington Made the Rich Richer and Turned Its Back on the*

Middle Class (Simon & Shuster, 2010), by political scientists Jacob Hacker and Paul Pierson.

They wanted to know how the U.S. became a society so unconscious, corrupted and starkly divided.

"Step by step," they write, "and debate by debate America's public officials have rewritten the rules of American politics and the American economy in ways that have benefited the few at the expense of the many."

As the rich and powerful got richer and more powerful, they bought off the gatekeeper, got inside and gamed the system. They owned and operated the government, "saddling Americans with greater debt, tearing new holes in the safety net, and imposing broad financial risks on Americans as workers, investors, and taxpayers." Hacker and Pierson, warn us the United States is looking more and more like "the capitalist oligarchies, like Brazil, Mexico, and Russia," where most of the wealth is concentrated at the top while the bottom grows larger and larger with everyone in between just barely getting by.

Historically this economic stage is the setting for social revolutions, liberations of the people, because extreme imbalance cannot be sustained.

The occupations and marches for fairness are the ushering in of a new era.

Big business and their big governments won't rejuvenate quality of life in your local community. It will be your community's investment in itself that circulates prosperity in new and inventive ways.

Everything is energy and the economy is exchanges of energy. New ways to barter, time bank, and exchange goods and services are happening. We're sharing the best new ideas at ConsciousWorldSummit.com.

Of course every place can't make everything. Trade and importing will continue, but all economics is local. If the people around you are unconscious, unproductive and poor, you'll be worse off too.

If your community doesn't have a healthy market for locally produced goods, your resources, wealth and potentials are bleeding away to the brands and big chain stores of the 1%.

We, the 99%, are now regaining Consciousness and realizing how much we've all suffered from greed-fueled capitalism's extreme globalization.

Many iconic American brands have been sold to foreign interests, particularly the Chinese, so the profits don't even stay in the country.

Budweiser is owned by Belgians and Purina is part of Swiss brand giant, Nestlé.

Chrysler's management is controlled by the Italian car company Fiat.

In 2005, 7-Eleven became an official subsidiary of the Japanese company, Seven & I Holdings.

Gerber is part of Swiss pharmaceutical giant, Novartis. Alka-Seltzer was purchased by the German company Bayer.

The British/Dutch conglomerate Unilever, bought the Vaseline brand and all the Best Foods brands like Hellman's Mayonnaise. In 2000, they also quietly purchased Ben & Jerry's.

The list goes on.

The purchase of the IBM ThinkPad brand by China-based Lenovo and the buyout of Firestone by Japan-based Bridgestone are more examples of how many big brands don't just siphon wealth out of your community, it leaves the country!

This doesn't begin to take into account the vast shareholdings that China bought during the crash of 2008.

When profits leave your community and your continent, the economies of whole nations drop through the system's cracks.

In 2011, ABC News reporter David Muir went into an average American home and removed everything that wasn't made in the U.S.A. Only one thing remained; a flower vase.

We've all enriched the 1%, at the cost of our own community.

How Do We Rejuvenate?

To get out of poverty, we've each got to climb the socio-economic ladder by offering something our community wants.

But where's the ladder?

Those franchises and chain stores of the globalized economy lured us to mindlessly buy and borrow. Lifestyles of the rich and famous became the American dream's enticing lure.

That dream's bubble burst into a nightmare.

We'd been so busy stuffing up our homes with foreign goods, that we hardly know what year community died. We hadn't noticed that the local community's economic ladder was gone, because we believed local progress was those big stores filled with trendy colored items from far way.

According to social scientists, globalization gutted our local economies as it made us progressively unhappy.

The Greed of Globalization

Globalization has been the growth strategy for big business and the big governments they sponsor. It's a mass transfer of local resources and potentials from communities to the owners of corporations - the richest .025%.

Globalization wipes out local authority, innovation, entrepreneurs, and creative opportunity while it fosters one-industry regions and nations manipulated by shadow governments, financed by monstrously too-big-to-fail corporations.

In one-industry towns, the whole community is the minion of the corporation. It's communal rape.

Think about those huge and intimidating lobbies of corporations and you get a sense of how small and insignificant we're supposed to feel in their towering shadows.

Big business uses intimidating, militaristic and governmentally regulated bullying.

A vitally important eye-opening read is Naomi Klein's book, *The Shock Doctrine* (Metropolitan Books, 2008). In it we discover how militaries, bullying and torture are used to develop the planet with globalization's concrete, fast food and big box stores.

Corporations are trying to own the Earth's water, to patent seeds and all the crops they cross-pollinate with, and to completely control education and the media.

They don't want us, the dumbed down 99%, to have vibrant local economies and so they've even made our own city halls unfriendly to local business.

To continue their planet plundering profiteering, they need us to remain low consciousness, squabbling, petty, afraid, indebted and unaware.

It's the continuum of corporatized imperialistic colonization, and loss of self-determination that's gripped local wellbeing in a stranglehold of bigness for more than five centuries.

And now it's collapsing into its own greed.

The grow-the-GDP-at-all-costs strategy of global economists has left all of life worse off.

My survey of billionaires is that they're stressed, comparative, competitive, uneasy, addicted, miserable people.

They're owned by their persona's artificial image, their addictive striving and their museum quality stuff.

I've been in enough of their mansions to realize the happiest people there know what drawer the spoons are in, because they work and eat in the kitchens.

Laughter, ease, creativity, gratitude and joy are not at life's extremities.

Economic globalization has been the orgy of prevailing political parties around the westernized world. It's what wealth addicted big governments and political parties do now.

Greed-addicts are the extremists who believe that bigger is always better and that more is always more.

They simply can't leave well enough alone, and after many centuries, their empires are falling—just in time because Life can't sustain their plans for all of us.

Countries like India and China are drinking the kool-aid and cokes and fast adopting Americanized consumerism, values and low consciousness.

If the people of India or China consume, pollute and waste like Americans, we'll rapidly exhaust the planet from over harvesting and CO_2 exhaust!

Globalizing the big box stores, with all those imported things nobody really needs, is the source of many of our problems.

This economic collapse comes at a time when most of our lives are stuffed up with too much stuff.

The age of getting more stuff, to prop up our identities, has failed miserably and has ended. We're shifting from buying our feelings to learning how to authentically *be* the feelings our hearts desire.

The industrialized age of getting and having hasn't made us happy or healthy and it had to stop.

Social scientists have proven that the price for globalizing any village is local identity, creativity, opportunity and happiness.

The high consciousness hearts of life loving mothers know that human happiness thrives in nurturing, creative communities. Titans of industry, politicians and those nerdy, social climbing economists know it too!

They all escape themselves to breathe deeply and enjoy simpler serenity at their weekend homes, in idyllic villages that shun franchised chain stores.

They pride themselves on having the wealth to savor the same village simplicity that their globalizing economies destroy.

Inefficiencies of Sale

It's crazy! As big governments addictively push for "growth" through globalizing free trade agreements, we're exporting the same resources and products that we import!

We're flying tuna caught in U.S. waters to be processed and branded in Japan and then transported back to the U.S.. The British are using precious fuel to transport apples from England, to be waxed in South Africa, and then flown back to be sold in the country that grew them.

The U.S. and Great Britain are importing and exporting nearly identical quantities of identical potatoes, beef, grain, milk, coffee and sugar.

Ontario, Canada grows premium lamb and almost all of it is exported. The local markets are stocked with imported lamb.

Globalization's branding is not only tremendously wasteful, as it intensifies to our climate crisis with vast CO_2 emissions, it rips the heart, self-esteem, identity and economic ladders out of local communities. When virtually nothing in our homes is made in our own country, never mind our own community, how do we appreciate and energize local talents, resources and creativity?

We've forgotten that appreciation appreciates! Every city looks more and more like every city.

It's increasingly difficult to applaud globalization for its contributions to transportation jobs, import duties and maintaining world peace.

In this post peak oil world, the cost of extracting, processing and delivering oil increases; yet we're still squandering it to needlessly move things about the planet.

The Saudis are spending billions to drill offshore because their land reserves are being tapped out.

We've passed the planet's peak ability to provide cheap oil cleanly. Globalization's greatest beneficiaries are the oily 1%.

Look around you. Where are the local opportunities and career ladders for the innovators and young people of your community? Are your local politicians bought by big developers? Is your City Hall supportive of local entrepreneurs?

We're all getting better at recognizing the snakes, but in the midst of collapse, where are the ladders?

A Lost Generation

They're called 'a lost generation' because finding a career that wants them, and is a worthy place for their focus and commitment, is a crisis.

UNICEF's 2011 international survey of happiness, revealed American children to be the second unhappiest in the world. Great Britain has the unhappiest children—largely because of the pressures and stresses of social climbing.

'The lost generations' of young people can see civilization crumbling. It's been the news most of their lives.

They see their stressed, disappointed and unhealthy parents and grandparents. They wisely resist the pressures to abandon logic, reason and their higher Consciousness at the school house doors to join an industrial revolution that has toxically failed to create wellbeing.

They recognize that the very rules and thinking they're supposed to live by, are ravaging our planet. During the last quarter of the nineteenth century, the Industrial Revolution created extraordinary wealth at the top and excruciating misery at the bottom.

If we're not rejuvenating our local community, so our young can find fulfilling places to invest their life energies, what lures them is internet games, TV, drugs and gangs.

For the most conscious among them, working for a fickle corporation or a franchise store looks like a prison sentence. Some young people say they don't see much difference between signing on with a polluting corporation or the military, because they both kill quality of life.

To see a culture's values and circumstances look at its youth. The youth is a mirror of a society.

Globalized chain stores are the vampires of human potential, happiness and creative fulfillment.

Locally, do you have a lost generation of impoverished youth with no local socio-economic ladder to get a leg up? Keep in mind that you're counting on their productivity for your retirement.

I know a retired California teacher feeling helpless as he receives desperate phone calls from homeless graduates. Some cry because they can't face one more night on the streets.

With each imported, globally branded, franchised buy, we toss away our own community's identity, potentials and future.

After centuries of our ancestors sacrificing to build thriving communities, we're the first generations alien to the harvest, the balance of nature and the soil that sustains us.

History may look back on us as Earth's most greedy, indebted harvest addicts.

What the 1% do to the rest of us, we're all doing to our Earth's resources.

Bankrupt Financiers

Would you allow someone who annually earns $50,000, spends $95,000, and is $300,000 in debt to be your financial manager?

Probably not. But, if you're American, you do every year you pay federal taxes.

Those are the approximate income to debt ratios of the U.S. federal government. Many other countries are more upside down than that and virtually all of the big prevailing political parties borrow to maintain power.

Patriotism is not worshipping anthems, flags, brands or militarism—it's responsible stewardship for a nation's lands, air and waters and all the people alive and yet unborn.

Perhaps by the time we all understand that, patriotism will have to be replaced by planetism. As the planet's ability to host life declines, it gets clearer that we're all in this together.

We're in a great global paradigm shift.

Industrialization and even globalization have given us much to be grateful for, and now their extreme domination is ending.

Who knew that the global economy was so dependent on Americans buying imported things they had no way of paying for?

The global economy is a teetering house of toxic mortgages, loans and credit card abuse, so let's get real and stop expecting big business and the indebted big governments they control to rejuvenate quality of life in your community. The globalization agenda that global politics is totally mired in and indebted to, does just the opposite.

As Albert Einstein so wisely said, "No problem can be solved from the same level of consciousness that created it."

Einstein witnessed consciousness and understood how high consciousness creates quality of life and low consciousness collapses it.

Extremism is low consciousness.

The mainstream media, owned by a handful of the Rupert Murdoch class, distracts us all with the extremist antics of the politicians they finance. They've taught journalists, and the 99%, to believe politics is a competitive team sport rather than a collaborative forum guiding the future of quality of Life on Earth.

While we're dumbed down and rooting for our *team* of political extremists, the big business globalizing shadow government does its toxic bidding.

Snap out of it! Wake up! Regain Consciousness! Carefully study the game changing 2011 film Thrive (thrivemovement.com). It's lunacy to go on calling the richest 1% evil and greedy, and then hope they'll employ you in a fulfilling career.

We endorse them with every big brand purchase we make. The money you spend in chain stores and gas stations leaves your community. It's often in London that night. And it isn't returning!

Insanity is believing that big government will fix your local economy when there is no apparent way to fix their own economics!

The mysterious riddle of the Humpty Dumpty nursery rhyme is being answered. All the king's horses and all the king's men won't be able to put the old economy together again.

Thank goodness!

The pendulum of change is swinging away from bigness and back to local community.

It is lunacy to go on calling the richest 1% evil and greedy, and then hope they'll employ you in a fulfilling career.

Pointing fingers of blame at greedy corporations and hoping they'll hire more of us is crazy. We endorse them with every big brand purchase we make. We vote with every dollar.

Insanity is believing that big institutions will fix your local economy when there is no apparent way to fix their own economics!

The mysterious riddle of the Humpty Dumpty nursery rhyme is being answered. All the king's horses and all the king's men won't be able to put their old economy together again.

It's gone too far.

The pendulum of change is swinging away from bigness and back to local community.

In the beautiful film, "The Economics of Happiness", social scientists have documented that well-being flows through communities that maximize local enterprise and co-ops.

The globalization of the economy has eliminated jobs, unravelled communities, accelerated climate crisis, declined health and stressed life. When Japanese villagers leave their small communities and come to the U.S., their cancer rates skyrocket, because they've left a nurturing, organic, supportive and creative community.

The global economy's collapse is our blessing.

It's time to replace petty politicized patriotism with planetism, right there in your own community.

True patriotism is caring for the land, the air, the water and ALL the people. It isn't serving the selfish agendas of big business.

As we regain consciousness, we move into humanity's next chapter, and it has the potentials to be the best ever!

Consciousness Is The Cure

The formula for success is find a problem, and *be* the Solution.

We're now seeing the greatest and most rejuvenating global shifts of our lifetimes.

The momentum of The Arab Spring is spreading like seeds of freedom wildflowers.

We're seeing and being a new genus of revolution, and in the backwash of collapse our best era will dawn, village by village.

Social media and web sites like Conscious World Summit are functioning like the underground cabarets of Europe during World War II. Out of sight of the regimes, courageously conscious people gather, speak the truth and then organize to liberate communities from the chokehold of tyranny.

We're online with our own media and schools now and we're becoming a peaceful consumer revolt. We're shunning the revolting indifference of greed-addicted aristocracies and their dooming agendas by rejuvenating our local economies.

Women make almost 90% of the purchases in North America.

This is why the Dalai Lama has said, the world will be saved by the western woman.

Buying from a locally owned business, rather than a chain store, keeps three times the wealth circulating in your community. One hundred dollars spent at a local book store contributes $45 to the local economy. Of $100 spent at the chain store, only $13 stays local.

According to the research firm Civic Economics, for every $1 million in revenue, chain restaurants employ 9.7 people while independent restaurants employ 14.8.

Buying local, creates three times the income effects and four times as many jobs throughout communities.

Local business keeps the salaries of upper management circulating within your community, as it supports local accountants and attorneys, local advertising and community programs.

Virtually none of this is supported by the chain stores.

The Great Recession teaches us that big business bleeds money from the quality of life of our communities and moves it into the mansions and mega yachts of the international 1%.

Let's prioritize quality of life in our own communities, so we're all free to create and prosper within our communities.

Our Community of Consciousness already represents the values shift of more than 80 million Americans already supporting local vendors, organic farmers and buying holistic and green products from conscious commerce. We're the grass roots movements for localization that are sprouting up through cracks in a crumbling economy.

The new definition of progress isn't coating the planet in asphalt, franchises and big box stores, it's growing local solutions right there close to your home.

The rapid growth of farmer's markets, street fairs and places to sell local creations is evidence of the wave.

Local business supports local suppliers that hire family and friends that support the locally owned hardware store and restaurants. A healthy local economy maintains real estate values and quality of life in a community.

All economics is local economics, let's care about quality of life for our grandchild's child and collectively support conscious commerce.

The pendulum of change is swinging back, away from being malled to death by franchises and big box stores and back to the warmth of living in a healthy greener human village.

As you've noticed, this book is about healing our souls and our material world with the awakening of higher Consciousness.

Work is the soul made visible.

In the aftermath of this great global shift, there will be freedom from tyranny, simplification, a more peaceful, harmonious Oneness, and living at the pace of Life.

The largest population in the history of the Earth, 7 billion human souls are here to march for, buy for and vote for the end of military/industrial/

corporate war with Life. The era of the Illuminati's tyranny is ending village by village.

We're the end of the dark ages and the dawn of a new relationship with *being*.

Homemade, locally grown, green, and organic are the signs of prosperity for our future. Every green product on the shelves is there because conscious people put them there. They need mothers and grandmothers to support them. Whenever someone looks into your refrigerator, they're seeing how conscious you are.

Be the change and join the Community of Consciousness!

With your participation, our best is yet to come.

How Consciousness Creates

Many of the new awakenings about how energy and consciousness create, come from the paradigm shifting discoveries of quantum physics.

For many graduate students of quantum physics there is a freak-out phase, when they have to find the courage to put their feet on the floor and stand up in the morning.

They've looked into electron microscopes and seen that atoms are mostly space. They've seen that everything our world is composed of, the soil, air, water, whatever you're sitting or lying on, your clothes, your skin and body, is more space than mass.

Empty space is anything but empty.

Science now perceives a Presence orchestrating atoms and molecules and our whole planet with a morphing, evolving form that's more like unset jello than rock. And they've realized that we observers influence how quantum energies align.

We are co-creators.
Here is a definition for a new paradigm.

Consciousness | 'kän ch əsnəs | noun

The orchestrating, architectural presence of everything.

Oneness with Creation's Presence.

Creation's Consciousness is the largest element of every tangible thing you know. It is the largest presence in our Universe.

Everything that is alive radiates a Presence of Consciousness.

When we open our hearts and minds to grateful oneness with Creation in this moment as this moment, painful illusions of separation, punishment and alienation melt away and we're open to Love Loving Life in a whole and healed way.

To feel it more, try relaxing and then expanding your mind, the energy in and around your brain. Then expand the Consciousness of your heart and connect mind and heart; try that now. After you've done this reread the previous paragraph.

The more your mind and heart are open and enlightened, the more Consciousness you're *being*.

We are Creation's dream; it is *being* us as we're *being* it.

Delusions of separation from Creation, because of space or time, are humanity's tragic folly. We had to be carefully taught by political and religious aristocracies. We were taught to *be* the industrial revolution with noses to the grindstones. We're supposed to ignore each dawning day and the beautiful garden of Life all around us.

We had to be industrialized into unconscious service. Humans are Life's worst and greatest possibility for itself.

Our Community of Consciousness

We're already the largest social movement of our time. Globally we're the peaceful, rejuvenating majority.

We know the same old institutions can't rejuvenate quality of life, so our community asks courageous questions that invite change and inspire greatness.

We're a quiet consumer revolt lifting the consciousness of commerce and government by saying, "no thanks" to low consciousness.

We're the rebellion against fake, poorly made and throwaway products. We're supporting organic foods, clean and free energy, holistic health care, conscious products, services and rejuvenation.

We're leaders of sustainable rejuvenation that's lifting us up and out to green, fertile, sustainable choices far beyond grubby, unconscious business as usual.

We're the 80 million Americans who've already created a $290 billion dollar U.S. economy of conscious products and services.

We're creating a beautiful net
of higher Consciousness,
preparing to catch the fall,
so we may all bounce back
better than before.

We're stepping out of the dark ages into the easy, comforting warmth of enlightenment.

The more Consciousness we're *being* the more creativity, sustainable solutions, community, gratitude, Love, synchronicity, flow and well-being we open through and unto ourselves.

We've already begun a new chapter, a new age. We are the phoenix of a new paradigm.

The era for polarizing aristocracies to alienate humanity from that peaceful knowing and Presence has ended.

Our global climate crisis aligned with economic and governmental collapse, is the renaissance of Life's greatest possibilities for itself.

It has to get bad enough for people to change.

As our climate crisis reveals the planet's pneumonia and as stubbornly addicted institutions of the old paradigm collapse into the greed of tyrannical aristocrats, our age of Oneness, humility, gratitude, Love, peace and possibility is dawning.

We're taking the best of the agricultural, industrial and information ages to co-create the greatest renaissance the world has known.

If your heart doesn't feel good, join us to try simple techniques that easily enlighten up your *being*, so fear, worry and alienation release their stranglehold on your spirit.

What's Happening?

We're now living the days of reckoning for centuries of left-brained, greed-addicted, materialistic unconsciousness. What's happening now is a global intervention.

We've been addicted to believing that having more is happiness, and we're recovering from centuries of escalated substance abuse.

We're not human havings, we're human beings. Being greed is the black hole to well-being that time and again collapses quality of relationships, quality of life, and entire civilizations.

Revered physicist Konstantin Korotkov has scientific evidence that gratitude expands energies in life-enhancing, creative ways—and that greed contracts Life energies into dark chaos. In an interview for a film viewable on consciousworldsummit.com he said, "This is why the former government of the Soviet Union collapsed. It was cruel, greedy and unsympathetic."

> History does not repeat itself, unconscious people repeat history.

Needy, greedy low consciousness is the vibrational energy of dog-eat-dog business values. It cultures resentment, jealousy, anger, worry, emptiness, addiction, struggle, fear and conflict, war and destruction.

Greedy, needy ego is the insatiable black hole of empty unconsciousness. Without higher Consciousness we become a needy, emotional, nervous, impulsive, messy mass. We come undone.

Consciousness Composes Life

We now have a science of Consciousness, a science that barely existed at the end of the last century. Today the courageous scientists, featured in this book and short films on ConsciousWorldSummit.com, are playing in the world championships of human history. They're giddy with astounding new evidence. Their discoveries open a new relationship with how Life creates itself. It ushers in a whole new paradigm.

Courageous and enlightened practitioners of new science and medicine are gathering, sharing, playing nicely together and embracing ancient wisdoms with statements like these:

"Every object in the Universe, including each elementary particle has consciousness."

Piero Scaruffi
cognitive scientist, Harvard and Stanford

"Life and space are like unset jello. Even the largest molecules in the Universe, 'buckyballs' are still unfinished."

Lynne McTaggart
author The Field and The Intention Experiment

"The Universe is a repository of knowledge that we have access to and upon which consciousness has control."

Henry Stapp
physicist, Lawrence Berkeley National Laboratory

"We're beginning to catch up...beginning to understand now things that we know in our hearts are true but we could never measure."

Dr. Mehmet Oz
physician, author, broadcaster

"The Universe functions like a consciousness-influenced floating hologram."

Dr. Carl Pribram
eminent neurosurgeon

The global shift we're experiencing includes a prolonged economic ratcheting down and climate crisis followed by an awakening to the awareness that we each co-create Life at profound levels. It will have to get bad enough for the mass consciousness to realize that without higher Consciousness we're chaos imploding quality of Life into a black hole of greedy, instant gratifications.

Konstantin Korotkov is a brilliant pioneer of this new science. For our "How Greed Destroys", film he said, "The science of consciousness is opening new concepts of what Life is and how we are all interacting with collective consciousness.

"We all contribute to collective consciousness.

"Consciousness and the collective consciousness is the transforming force of human history.

"Consciousness is a material representation of Love.

The global shift is Life saving Life.

Our Community of Consciousness redefines what living *the good life* is. We awoke from a bad dream of blind loyalty to big greedy brands and now we're supporting the consciousness of regional green economies.

A simple, good, comfortable life in a peaceful, conscious community is *the good life*.

The U.S. economic and real estate bubble at the dawn of this century were the years corporate greed bushwhacked us. That was also when international surveys of happiness rated Americans, a people addictively borrowing to have and to hoard, among the less happy people on the planet.

The happiest included the families of Bangladesh, people who possessed almost nothing other than their joy, Love of living each day as gratitude, and Gandhi's teachings of sustainable happiness through higher Consciousness.

The lesson is that we aren't grateful because we're happy, we're happy because we're grateful.

My Cocktail Party Epiphany

In 2007 I'd found a way to open my BEing through gratitude. It lifted me to a profound peace, a creative flow, and a beautiful new way of being. Regardless of where I was or the circumstances around me, I was uncharacteristically at peace. I didn't need anything external to experience sustainable bliss and well-being. This changed everything for me, and as I researched to more fully understand it, I dropped off the social radar.

Five years later, after writing what you're now reading I socially resurfaced at a southern California cocktail party.

I was mingling, swizzling and sizzling when someone I barely recognized blurted, "What's happened with you?!"

"What do you mean?" I asked.

"We haven't seen you for a long time. You've found something. You're different!"

I had. And I was. But I didn't know it showed.

"I want to know...really!" he asked.

He seemed sincere, so I responded.

"I found a portal up to higher Consciousness."

His eyes widened and waited.

"I now feel the presence of Creation in everything."

"You saw God!" He turned and motioned for his party playmate to come over.

"You were right," he said to his eager friend. "He saw God!"

"Well," I replied "I wouldn't put it..."

"Okay where is God?" asked the friend, as if God still owed him money. "What did you see?"

I hadn't really known either of these people. They'd been extras in "The Scene." We'd exchanged two or three lines of dialogue at various social productions.

"Come on, don't hold back... tell us!"

They looked deeply into my eyes, anxious, anticipating, sensing that I am something I wasn't before.

"I didn't see," I explained.

Three more people slipped within hearing range. Then suddenly there were six.

Apparently talking about this had a mysterious attraction—and the ability to hush even those more gaudy than Godly.

"I didn't see an entity or superpower. I found a way to open my presence, my BEing. What I do is feel the presence of my BEing, my Life force energies, and I open my gratitude for BEing. I expand that presence of gratitude and open it to the presence of everything that IS. Up where there's no judgment, no separation... and I become blissful peace."

They gawked.

So, I reviewed.

"We can get there by opening our heart's gratitude for BEing. By opening our presence and connecting it with the Presence of All of Creation just as it is now... without judgment, just gratitude."

And on I continued.

"Opening my presence to *be* a peaceful oneness with the presence of everything, without judgments healed my Life."

"What if we only have to appreciate the beautiful joy of being, without judgment, comparing or competing?"

"Being that peace, my Life is spectacular, it's more than I could have expected or imagined. Just surrender to being the joy and allow that to guide you!"

The party gaggle gawked.

Uh-oh! Had I really just poured that truth into this social Cuisinart?

Why did I break open like that?

I lifted my eyes to face the jury.

And I saw them.

I saw their presence, their ageless childlike awe.

The older, more grounded people glowed with a warm, beautiful ageless smile.

Yes, younger ones had it too.

Some sweet tears of gratitude glistened in the eyes.

Time stopped and there was oneness.

Someone offered a heartfelt "Thank you."

Another, "Beautiful." She sighed and wiped a tear, saying to no one in particular, "I got there."

"I did too," responded another.

"We all felt it," said an older gentleman.

"You felt it?" I asked.

"I did."

"So," I pondered, "other people can feel it too?"

"You're onto something, McGugan."

"Yes, he's found something," someone else replied.

I felt the Cosmic calm, the sublime oneness.

More than just the attracted luck of being in the right place at the right time, this transcended place, time and limitation. That moment of accepting that we—that all humanity—could experience and *be* this bliss together lifted me.

It was at that party that I first experienced our readiness for the new paradigm and the Community of Consciousness.

Yet I could not have imagined that night just how fearlessly ready I'd need to be for transformational loss.

That night I wasn't aware that, because of what shuts down the hearts of humanity, absolutely nothing is for sure.

Welcome To Our Renaissance

Something is changing everything; millions of us feel it.

The Aquarian age of social media is liberating us to stealthily organize social movements that liberate Life from hellishly greedy regimes.

Tyrants can no longer subdue us with a stranglehold on publishing, media, education, religion or weapons.

We're taking to the streets and to the stores, where it really impacts.

The global village has arrived; it's a social media linked Renaissance of Consciousness that's lifted by new revelations about how greed-addicted men have rigged societies and how Creation orchestrates Life.

This book's first three chapters offer the kinds of proof that left-brained, prove-it people need.

I count myself among them.

I want my beliefs to be born through experiences, reason and logic.

The search continues to lead me to amazing conversations, communities, insights and profound confirmations.

I seek discoveries and experiences that courageous, respected explorers have published in peer-reviewed journals.

Some are like the scholars interviewed in the 2008 documentary film "Expelled: No Intelligence Allowed."(Rocky Mountain Pictures, 2008). Because they crossed a line and cited a Life orchestrating omnipresence, an intelligent design, they were shunned and expelled from colleges and universities dependent on funding from the old paradigm aristocracy. The 1% demands science stays inside their box.

But the internet and social media are blowing the walls off the box and pulling back the curtains to expose the truth of higher Consciousness and the dark, unconscious wizards of our Oz.

As I write this, exciting new awakenings come from fringe science. But as we're now seeing throughout our culture, what was a holistic fringe is centering to enlighten and heal us, while old paradigm institutionalized beliefs and agendas are fraying into antiquated thinking.

The old rules that licensed us to live unconsciously, follow the leaders and rape our planet are passing into oblivion.

Consciousness is Identity

It brings us home again.

We are much more than thoughts and emotions, much more than we've been taught to believe. We are something else!

We are our authentic Presence of Consciousness. And that's infinitely more connected and creative, fulfilling and eternal than just the need generating electricity of mind.

Consciousness is orchestrating every molecule of everything, and our essence is a brilliant concentration of Consciousness.

Everything throughout ALL of time has brought us to this crucial and teachable moment for humanity; this tipping point is our turning point. Our Community of Consciousness is taking the very best of the agricultural, industrial, and information ages to create local conscious commerce and our renaissance.

The global shift and the collapse of tyrannical regimes marks the end of the isolating, shark-eat-shark, dark ages of unconscious greed.

Broken Open

We're all broken open, humbled and teachable.

We're at a global threshold of choice. It's time to reflect.

The choice is whether to continue to be unconscious and part of the problem, or to awaken and learn to *be* Life's solution for itself.

There is no new normal.
And that is our opportunity.

It has to get bad enough for people to change.

We'll change to get from a place of pain to a better place we're convinced is less painful. Nations, cultures, corporations, communities and families broke open with this shift.

Collapsed to our knees, we realize we've got to begin to begin again in a new and better way.

The shift that hit the ego's plan is Creation saving Life from being sucked into a black hole of greed.

There are 7 billion of us here to witness the revelations of this Earth awakening.

We've got more help than we know.

It won't be the end of the world. It will end the pain of a cancerous, greed addicted aristocracy—a small group that believes fewer people are easier than communities of higher Consciousness.

We must awaken higher Consciousness now.

Something is changing everything; it's the dawn of a new paradigm, a natural-is-better, wise, respectful, compassionate and sensible (sense-abled) way of appreciating and *being* alive.

It's Life saving itself.

New Paradigms

Our paradigms, our understanding and relationship with BEing, have been carefully programmed into us based on values, models and theories licensed by the aristocracies.

We're now realizing that what we are *being*, Life becomes.

We are not human havings, human doings or human consumings, we are human *beings*.

We're free when we shift from buying our feelings, to authentically *being* the feelings the wisdom of our hearts desire.

The change is happening within us.

The global shift is an intervention of Consciousness that's breaking addictions to getting.

For our film in the New Economy section of ConsciousWorldSummit.com, cofounder of The Human Potential Movement , Dr. Jean Houston said, "We've come to the end of *the having* and I think because of dire necessity by the Earth's needs, we are stepping into *BEingness*."

Quality of Consciousness
creates quality of experience.

If our agendas remain addicted to instant
gratifications, easy quality of Life on Earth is
doomed.
We have been the seventh generations again
and again. What we leave behind in this lifetime is
what we'll inherit in the next—if our Mother Earth
can host us at all.
If she can't, what place would have us?

Free Will's Choice

You can lurch through the days as
unconsciousness.
You can be a functionary, behaving more like an
industrial machine than a conscious BEing.
You can attract people functioning at your same
levels and have low consciousness relationships
and experiences.
You can earn a low consciousness living and
barely exist. Gratitude, fulfillment, confidence, a
Love of Life and peace will elude you. You'll have
sold your soul for some stuff, and your ego-driven,
steel-hearted discontent will lead you to
addictions, disillusionment, conflicts and a fright-
filled future.
The industrial revolution was a terrifically
overwhelming success, virally infecting everything
from language, time, spirituality and education to
well-being. But now, the same marauding
industrialization we were taught would always
sustain us, is often a cancer weakening quality of
life.

Prescription For A Dying Paradigm

"I'm not feeling at all well," the patient said to the HMO doctor.

"What are you feeling?"

"I do a meaningless job and feel stressed, I see the news and feel terrorized. I eat and feel polluted and I can't get a good night's sleep. I haven't worked in a week!"

"O.K., here," said the doctor as he handed the patient a preprinted prescription.

"What is it?"

"A tranquilizer. Something to stop the stress."

"That's not my solution!"

"O.K., I'll double the dosage."

If you continue playing by aristocratic-old-school rules you'll be lost among the dumbed down, drugged and dragging dysfunctionally normal.

Wake up, normal is gone!

Addiction hides itself. The euphoric highs and the culture of the addiction desensitize the users from their addiction's diabolical progressions.

The substance abuse, and its clandestine culture, become the abusing addict's community, and this is why a powerful intervention, an undeniably awakening event is needed to snap the addict out of it long enough for them to see and be freed from the addiction's chokehold.

By being higher Consciousness, addicts enlighten the black energy hole of their hearts and are freed to recover their clarity and joyfully Loving hearts.

At higher energy realms of Consciousness, creativity, hope, health, happiness and Love blossom.

We've all been living in an addictive culture of getting, having and hyper-consuming. And like addicts, we barely experience what we're consuming.

That food on your dinner plate grew from our Earth's soil. It's energized by the Sun, rain, atmosphere and soil, and it passes Creation's Consciousness to you and through you. Pure Creation composes you. It is you.

You're eating God's designs, scents and flavors. We're living in a Cosmic garden of Earthly delights, a magnificent garden of Eden.

That food on your dinner plate took months to grow for you, and yet most of us are too rushed and stressed to give it much notice or to share in the gratitude.

We're the privileged generations experiencing a whole magnificent garden of Earthly delights and because we have so much of everything, we barely notice or appreciate anything.

Addiction is like this. It numbs the addict until insatiable getting is the only sensation left.

The Great Recession is the intervention reawakening the sensations and appreciation of masses of people.

One gift of loss is that our ability to feel Life is aroused. Loss is the intervention that reminds us of what isn't important and what didn't really matter or make us feel validated, Loved and gratefully at peace with being.

This book is an intervention that opens higher Consciousness so we may revitalize quality of life in our communities and on this planet.

It's high time for higher mass consciousness.

The wounded heirs of ultimate wealth are wielding their power, and everyone is called upon to *be* their compassionate interventionists.

An extremely addicted and powerful elite believes that our societies, as they are, cannot be sustained. Rather than shift from fossil fuels, to new free energy technology and to higher Consciousness, they believe massive depopulation is the best solution and they're preparing for it.

A great intervention of higher Consciousness has begun. Our calling is to help the power elite, and their unquestioning military personnel, snap out of this fearful and diabolically addicted mindset.

With higher Consciousness and the new energy technology, that is being held back, we can all thrive with Life.

Our whole Universe is aligned for humanity's next great Renaissance.

The end of The Dark Ages and our Great Global Spring has begun.

What was the Earthy and green social fringe is becoming mainstream, and the old conspicuously all-consuming normal is frayed and dismayed.

The old school paradigms and global domination mindsets are looking more and more like addictive, egocentric mental disorders.

Every crisis is a crisis of unconsciousness.

Consciousness is the very thing we're searching for, so let's understand it.

CHAPTER 1

Consciousness and Well-being

Take a breath. The change happens within us. This chapter explores scientific awakenings. It shows us the more Consciousness holds Presence in your body and your Life, the healthier, happier and more Divinely connected and protected you are.

"Our thinking influences moment-by-moment cell reproduction."

Dr. Candace Pert
neuropharmacologist, author

In her best selling book, *The Molecules of Emotion*, Dr. Candace Pert explained that your body is creating 300,000,000 new cell divisions every minute and these cells retain aspects of the energy you're *being* as they're created.

Higher Consciousness creates healthier, more organized and robust cells, while *being* hate, fear and chaos creates cellular chaos.

Quality of Consciousness influences quality of health.

Westernized medicine has begun to understand the Creation Consciousness that orchestrates the creation, rejuvenation and intelligence in the new cells we create every hour, and all Life on Earth.

The Heart's Song

There have been many documented cases of heart recipients adopting the preferences, tastes, habits, interests and talents of the person whose heart they received—a heart donor they'd never met and about whom they knew nothing.

Dr. Gary Schwartz, author of The God Experiments, is an avid researcher of systemic and cellular memory. He recounts the story of a seven-year-old girl who received the heart of a murdered woman. In her dreams the girl began seeing a murder with specific details. She was terrified.

Her mother took her to a psychiatrist who came to the conclusion that it was too detailed to be just a fear.

They took the girl to the police and it was through her dream recollections that they were able to identify and bring the murderer to justice.

Stories like this have been documented in the books, The Heart's Code: Tapping the Wisdom and Power of Our Heart Energy, by Paul Pearsall, and The Living Energy Universe: A Fundamental Discovery that Transforms Science and Medicine, by Gary E. Schwartz and Linda G. Russek.

Dr. Schwartz is being funny when he says:

> "Obviously it works in practice,
> but does it work in theory?"
>
> Dr. Gary Schwartz

Consciousness defies many traditional theories.

When we witness heart-retaining memory, talents and cellular awareness, our minds are invited to open and to understand that what, how and who we are *being* is absorbed in the cells of our bodies.

The Lightness of Being

All living things are like candles emitting tiny particles of light. This light of Life energy is like a supreme high-frequency laser of photons.

In the Soviet Union these biophoton emissions are being measured to diagnose the complete spectrum of health issues. Dr Konstantin Korotkov of Saint Petersburg, Russia, discovered that if you flash a living thing with lots of light, the way the sun does, you excite the electrons, and they absorb and then generate light that you can capture on film. He's created computerized systems that allow us to read and diagnose these photon emissions, particularly to see energy deficiencies in highly specific mental and physical areas.

This is being used to diagnose disease, to diagnose athletic potential for Russian Olympic athletes, and to evaluate the effectiveness of homeopathic substances. The diagnostic accuracy is 90-95 percent.

Dr. Korotkov has observed that, in states of higher Consciousness, people open and increase the flow of energy meridians, particularly in the realms of higher and more refined ultraviolet frequencies.

He also measured evidence of Consciousness before, during and after death. Consciousness declines at the moment of death and diminishing traces of it linger around the body, occasionally up to four days. [1]

The orchestrating essence of a being survives after death.

rotkov writes: "Our consciousness is part
ne spark that exists not just at the
t but long after our death. We are not just
organs and systems packed in a body, we are
much more than that. We are energy, we are Sun,
we are Light, and our consciousness allows us to
be connected to higher spheres, and higher
dimensions."

Qi is Creation Consciousness

Qi | ch ē | (also chi) noun

The circulating life force whose
existence and properties are the basis
of much Chinese philosophy and
medicine.

Qigong (pronounced 'chegung') was developed
around 5000 BC, making it the world's oldest
energy medicine. The name means "cultivating life
energy." It is the energy awareness and practice
closest to how my audio programs teach you to
embody and *be* Creation Consciousness.

In the 1960s the Shanghai Institute of
Hypertension began a long-term study of more
than 240 people with high blood pressure. Half
the people did 30 minutes of Qigong twice a day,
while the others did not.

Thirty years later there were half as many
deaths and half as many strokes among the
people who practiced Qigong. [2]

Research has proven that Qigong lowers the
stress hormone cortisol and enhances
T-lymphocytes in white blood cells by up to 50
percent, thus causing a marked increase in
cytokines (immune-regulating substances).
These are major elements of the body's natural
immune and healing systems.

The Infinite Mind
of Consciousness

Herbert Benson, M.D., is the founding president of the Mind/Body Medical Institute and an associate Professor of Medicine at the Harvard Medical School. He was astonished that Tibetan monks who practice Tum-mo yoga could lower their metabolism by up to 64 percent. Most people's maximum drop in metabolic rate is only 10 to 15 percent during sleep.

These Consciousness practitioners proved in a clinical study that they're able to pull energy from the atmosphere to survive situations that would kill the rest of us. When wet sheets were placed on their naked bodies, in near freezing temperatures, the monks were able to pull Universal energy and raise their skin temperatures by 17 degrees, thus drying the sheets!

"It serves as a striking demonstration of the awesome power of the human mind," says Dr. Benson.

The monks open their energy torus and focus its heat generating ability.

We live in an action-packed atmosphere of energy and the new free energy technology will open its availability to each of us.

Scientists claim there is enough energy in a cubic foot of our atmosphere to boil an ocean and soon we'll have local people building free energy devices that extract energy from the fabric of space around us. This energy cannot be metered and it will end the greed-addicted, evil tyranny of the energy elite.

Our wireless phones and computers use the ability of our atmosphere to transport and hold information. With an opened mind acting like a satellite dish flowing Consciousness, we can pull vast amounts of energy, knowledge and wisdom.

Case after case proves that lifting awareness out of our minds and up into the realms of Consciousness lifts us into the realms of superhuman energies.

Superhuman Energies

Has a mother ever actually lifted a car off her trapped child?

Witnesses and The Associated Press say that, on April 9, 1982, Angela Cavallo of Lawrenceville, Georgia, did just that.

Angela's teenage son Tony had a 1964 Chevy Impala jacked up in the driveway to remove a rear tire. When a neighbor kid came to the kitchen door to tell Angela there'd been an accident, she rushed out to find Tony pinned under the car. Something had gotten stuck, and in trying to loosen it, he'd rocked the car off the jack. Now he was partially caught from the waist up under one of the rear wheel wells.

While hollering to the neighbor kid to get help, Angela grabbed the side of the car with both hands and summoned the strength to lift it for five minutes. The 1964 Chevy Impala is a full-sized car weighing 3340 lbs (1,515 kg).

The AP account said she raised the car four inches; enough to take the pressure off until two neighbors reinserted the jack and dragged the boy out. Tony recovered.

The sight of her son pinned under a car sent Angela into the realms of pulling unlimited energy.

Angela, then in her late 50s, recalls nothing about the rescue. This is a common trait of those who have "gone out of their mind" and up into the realms of pure Consciousness, pure Universal energy. We can make our will a laser instantly vaporizing limitations of belief and become pure superhuman energy.

Tom Boyle did it in Tucson. He saw a boy hit by a car, then pinned underneath it. He later told the Arizona Daily Star he couldn't believe what he saw. "Oh my God. You think things like that only happen in movies." Boyle took action. He lifted the front end of the Chevrolet Camaro up high enough so the driver could pull 18-year-old Kyle Holtrust away. Then Boyle held the teen until help arrived.

"All I could think is, what if that was my son," Boyle said. "I'd want someone to do the same for him."

Tom received an American Red Cross Real Heroes Award in 2007.

Energies available to us for drawing strength, ability, and healing are vast.

The Consciousness Healers

For his doctoral thesis, California clinical and forensic psychologist Allan Cooperstein studied 20 people famous for being highly effective energy healers. What distinguishes them, he learned, is an ability to merge with the sea of Consciousness. This is described by some as an "energy sea," by others as a connection with spiritual BEing, and by still others as extra-human abilities manifesting through them.

Most doctors of conventional western medicine diagnose with and trust their gut, intuition, and higher Consciousness as well as the medical school programming in their brains. They take in information about symptoms, and after a period of silence—perhaps taking a long, deep breath and moving their awareness within—they form a diagnostic sense of things.

A common trait among famous energy healers who openly use Universal or Creation Consciousness energy to heal is a willingness to open their conscious mind to what they consider a great healing force beyond themselves.

Claims that people can project healing energies were proven by the Guangzhou University of Medical Sciences and published in North American peer-reviewed journals. Two Qigong Masters reduced the infection rates of laboratory rats exposed to a severe pneumonia virus by an average of 60 per cent.

When these Qigong Masters were asked to focus their Life force energies on test tubes of human white blood cells for only one minute, they were able to increase the cells' regeneration rates by 59 percent. [3]

The American Journal of Chinese Medicine, reported in 2001 that Qigong Masters made another type of immunity boosting cells twice as effective by directing qi energy into them. [4]

In a similar experiment (this one not formally published in a peer reviewed journal), doctors at the University Hospital of Ghent, Belgium, invited a Qigong Master to attempt to reduce the size of tumors in mice infected with cancer cells.

The treated mice lived longer and had tumors, on average, half the size of the mice untreated with Qigong. These experiments eliminate the placebo effect of a human patient's expectations.

Measurements of the energy pulled by Qigong's healing practitioners show they generate a highly refined electromagnetic energy field from either their head or hands—up to 1000 times stronger than the usual human electromagnetic field. [5]

They also emit strong infrasonic waves (sounds too low to be audible to humans). [6]

In theory, a patient pulling Creation Consciousness energy (chi) could energize the healing of virtually any medical condition.

Renowned American energy healer, Dr. Eric Pearl has impressed many respected scientists with the quantifiable healing techniques he's taught to more than 65,000 people around the world. Featured in the documentary *The Living Matrix: A Film On the New Science of Healing* (Beyond Words Publishing 2009), Dr. Pearl's reconnective healing process reopens and unblocks people so natural healing can happen.

Dr. Konstantin Korotkov has measured the energy influences of Dr. Pearl and his students with instruments highly sensitive to changes in the energy structure, the entropy of space.

Dr. Korotkov confirms what other scientists have reported, the energy of their focused healing powers dramatically changes their environment. "You are not a little being just eating and sleeping," says Dr. Korotkov. "You are an active force of The Universe, and with your own Consciousness you can really change Life. You can make Life much better for yourself and everybody around you."

The Brain on Consciousness

Research by Daniel Goleman, the author of *Emotional Intelligence* (Bantam, 1995) and other books about science and meditation, shows us that the brains of meditators register bursts of high-frequency beta or gamma waves often associated with moments of "ecstasy."

Awareness is lifted to heightened perception without the emotional anchors of day-to-day stress.

By lifting ourselves above sludge-like emotions that pull us down, we're ascending to a higher, wiser viewpoint and opening ourselves to higher energy frequencies. These are proving to be the frequencies that energize cellular reproduction and healing.

Evidence from MRI tests show that brains of meditators are healthier and thicker, and more practice increases those benefits.

The brain's neocortex manages sight and hearing and while its health and thickness typically deteriorate with age, regular meditation reduces and often reverses the process. [7]

Consciousness Heals

Researchers at Harvard Medical School discovered meditation activates parts of the brain that control the autonomic nervous system. This consciousness system governs bodily functions over which the intentional mind has no control.

BEing higher Consciousness increases well-being as it heals digestion, blood pressure, and the heart—the emotion-vulnerable systems that still mystify westernized medicine.

Studies show that even simple meditation, that doesn't intentionally open the mind and heart to Consciousness, reduces the risk of heart attack by 11 per cent. And it reduces the risk of stroke by 8-15 per cent.

Among 60 people with fatty deposits in their arterial walls (atherosclerosis), simple meditation for nine months decreased the thickness of those walls, while the artery walls of non-meditators became thicker and more problematic. [8]

An analysis of US hospital records published by Psychosomatic Medicine revealed that regular meditators had half the hospital treatments of non-meditators in 17 different treatment categories. [9]

The benefits of meditation could be measured in the activities of the brain for up to four months after the meditating ended. Consciousness lingers.

Higher Consciousness activates an increase in cerebral blood flow and opens a mind-body connection. It's as though we've just opened the brain, mind and body flow.

Using standardized measures of aging (eyesight, hearing, and blood pressure) long-term meditators slow down their own aging process. People who'd been meditating longer than five years were physiologically as much as 12 years "younger" than their physical age. Even less experienced meditators showed increased youthfulness [10]

Still another study indicates meditation pro-longed the lives of 80-year-olds in retirement homes. They were happier and enjoyed life more. [11]

One reason for this change is a decrease in stress hormones. Just four months of meditation reduced the major stress hormone cortisol. [12]

Scientists previously believed that the brain essentially stopped changing after adulthood. However meditation actually enhances the structuring of the brain, especially in the regions responsible for sense of self, stress, memory and empathy. [13]

In 2011, a study conducted by Wake Forest Baptist University found that meditation could reduce pain intensity by 40 percent and pain unpleasantness by 57 percent. Morphine and other pain-relieving drugs typically show a pain reduction of 25 percent. [14]

Spending time meditating restores energy, allowing us to perform better at tasks that require attention and concentration.

But, wouldn't a midday nap work just as well?

No, says Bruce O'Hara, associate professor of biology at the University of Kentucky.

In a 2011 study, he had college students either meditate, sleep or watch TV. Then he tested alertness, asking them to hit a button when a light flashed. Meditators performed 10% better— "a huge jump, statistically speaking," says O'Hara. Those who snoozed did significantly worse.

Not surprisingly, given those results, Google and a growing number of corporations, offer meditation classes to their workers.

Making us think more clearly is only one benefit; studies also say meditation improves productivity, in large part by preventing stress-related illness and sick days.

Another benefit: meditation helps regulate emotions, which in turn helps people get along.

Richard Davidson, director of the Laboratory for Affective Neuroscience at the University of Wisconsin says, "One of the most important domains meditation acts upon is emotional intelligence—a set of skills far more consequential for life success than cognitive intelligence."

Stress: a black hole to well-being

Humans are the only species to choose constant stress over tranquility.

According to Harvard's Dr. Herbert Benson, "More than 60 per cent of visits to doctors are due to stress-related problems, most of which are poorly treated by drugs, surgery, and other medical procedures."

According to The Journal of Clinical Psychology, not only do simple forms of meditation de-stress us, they've been proven to beat burnout, save careers, marriages, and greatly enhance family dynamics. [15]

Marriage counsellors and addiction specialists cite numerous studies that have proven meditation to be one of the most effective ways of curing addictions.

A meditation study with 50 American inner city adolescents showed a marked drop in poor discipline and absenteeism. Other U.S schools found that IQ and exam performance can be improved by regular meditation. [16]

Social solutions are not in the extreme, they're at the center of the heart's higher Consciousness.

Neuroscientist Professor Owen Flanagan of Duke University wondered if the happiness, serenity and loving kindness of meditators creates fitness in the brain. The answer is yes, indeed!

The brains of Buddhist monks studied by MRI and positron emission tomography (PET) scans show, according to Flanagan, "persistent activity in the left prefrontal lobes." This area of the brain creates foresight, planning, and self-control, and is also involved with lighthearted, positive emotions.

The Consciousness of the Tibetan monks, observed not just while meditating, but throughout the day, created what Flanagan calls "the highest levels of activity we have ever seen in that area of the brain." In 2011 a study from Massachusetts General Hospital and Harvard Medical School proved that you don't have to be a Tibetan Monk to get the benefits.

Meditation aids in lowering blood pressure, improves immune system and brain function and minimizes pain sensitivity. It makes us smarter, more aware, healthier, quicker, more reliable and easier to live with.

Being higher Consciousness allows natural maintenance and healing to take place in everything from hearing to eyesight as well as in the brain, heart, arteries, attitude and relationships.

If all the research benefits are compiled, it increases health and emotional well-being overall by 60 percent! What else enhances wellbeing as completely as this?

Research supports meditating a few minutes twice a day, and that's why we've made it easy to listen to our various Mind Spa audio programs through your computer or smart phone at ConsciousWorldSummit.com.

The Mind Spa supports us through change, loss and grief, as it rejuvenates. It expands basic meditating by opening mind/body/being flow, and attuning us with higher Consciousness.

We look forward to the results of research into the broad benefits of our Mind Spa programs.

The standard equipment of every mortal mind is a built-in skylight that, when opened unto the higher realms of Creation's Consciousness, delivers the ethereal Presence of Creation flowing to and through everything.

When you hold Consciousness as your Presence, you truly arrive for your life.

The journey from mind
to higher Consciousness
is the shortest distance and the
ultimate destination.

CHAPTER 2

Oneness

W e only need to look at a photograph of our Mother Earth, as seen from space, to know that everything here on Earth is one unified entity.

Everything on Earth is
ONE Presence of Life.

For more than 700 years, there have been two distinct world-views or belief systems: one that considers everything as separate and mechanistic, and another that believes Life and Nature are one holistic presence. Because industrial machinists dominated the 20th century, their *nature be damned* industrial revolution was an overwhelmingly toxic success.

Personally I'm profoundly grateful for industrialization's clever ingenuity. I'm especially grateful for what central heating and air conditioning does for quality of life.

I'm not against industry, I'm for higher Consciousness in industry.

We're living in a time of addictive extremes, and it's high time for higher Consciousness because the days of reckoning for crimes against Nature and humanity are upon us.

Don't despair. Stay centered
Crisis pulls us together.

How Oneness Works

Let's look at practical, peer-reviewed, scientific evidence that collectively being the Oneness of higher Consciousness is Life's great hope for itself.

The pioneers of beingness—quantum physicists —have recently made discoveries that enlighten and refresh an open mind.

With every epiphany, they revalidate wisdom of our peaceful and harmonious ancestors who lived as Consciousness and related to the world through Oneness.

In 1935, Nobel prize-winning physicist Albert Einstein witnessed amazing elasticity and transformational presence in the details of quantum energy, and it defied what scientists had taught themselves to believe for the previous six centuries.

When Einstein witnessed human Consciousness influencing quantum energies, the door was opened only a crack. Now it's being flung wide open: solid, peer-reviewed, scientific evidence is literally changing beliefs and our way of being.

What we'd been taught is just empty space is actually intelligent energy filled with and orchestrated by Consciousness.

The agenda of Creation's Consciousness is to create more of itself through itself.

History has proven that organizatons that attempt to block or eradicate Nature's flow of Creation, collapse into their own chaos.

The Weave Of Entanglement

Two photons traveling at the speed of light in opposite directions from the atom that has emitted them retain an immediate nonlocal connection. When the polarization of one is measured, the other will instantly have the opposite polarization. This is known as quantum entanglement, and it can be witnessed at all levels of energy.

If connected in the past, parts of a system retain that connection even when far apart. Everything is energetically entangled!

Small blind termites, build complex 10-foot high nests with intricate tunnels, galleries, chambers, and ventilation shafts. Up to a million termites are able to work in harmony to co-create the structures. Their common understanding of the desired architecture is communicated through a cooperative Consciousness, as if the insects are of one mind. When a sudden repair is needed, the new mission is activated silently and almost instantly.

How do flocks of birds or schools of fish simultaneously change direction without individuals bumping into each other? Among fish, these mass movements happen in one-fiftieth of a second—too fast for nerve impulses to move from the eye to the brain and then from the brain to the muscles. Even temporarily blinded fish are still capable of joining and maintaining their position within the school. They have this instantaneous oneness of mind at night. The fish are operating in a state of simultaneous group Consciousness.

Films with extremely rapid exposures reveal
that flock movements among sandpipers originate
from a single bird and can be initiated from
anywhere within the flock. Individual birds
instantly assume leadership of the flock
movements from here to there, and "awareness"
of the directional changes takes only 15 thousands
of a second to pass from bird to bird—too fast for
the eye to coordinate muscle response. In lab
experiments these birds react to a flash of light in
38 thousandths of a second; more than twice the
flock response time. The flock maneuvers as one
flowing, dancing Presence of Consciousness.

All social animals are unified by morphic fields
of Consciousness—energies which maintain a
group oneness.

Feelings Are Infectious

Social research published in 2008 proved that
in a social network, happiness spreads among
people up to three degrees removed from one
another. That means when you feel happy, a
friend of a friend of a friend has a slightly higher
likelihood of feeling happy too.

The lesson is that taking control of your own
happiness can positively affect others, says James
Fowler, co-author of the study and professor of
political science at the University of California in
San Diego.

"We get this chain reaction in happiness that I
think increases the stakes in terms of us trying to
shape our own moods to make sure we have a
positive impact on people we know and love,"
he said.

The researchers found that sadness also
spreads in a social network, but not as quickly.
Each happy friend increases your own chance of

being happy by 9 percent, whereas each unhappy friend decreases it by 7 percent. This reflects the total effect of all social contacts.

The study found that you are 15 percent more likely to be happy if a direct connection is happy, 10 percent if the friend of a friend is happy, and 6 percent if it's a friend of a friend of a friend.

Fowler and co-author Dr. Nicholas Christakis of Harvard Medical School charted friends, spouses and siblings in the network, and used their self-reported happiness ratings from 1983 to 2003. The study was published in the British Medical Journal.

Daniel Todd Gilbert, professor of psychology at Harvard University and author of *Stumbling on Happiness* (Knopf, 2006), called the study "a stunning paper by two of the most respected scientists in the field". This was a statement broadcast by CNN.

"We've known for some time that social relationships are the best predictor of human happiness, and this paper shows that the effect is much more powerful than anyone realized," Gilbert said. "It is sometimes said that you can't be happier than your least happy child. It is truly amazing to discover that when you replace the word 'child' with 'best friend's neighbor's uncle,' the sentence is still true."

The study found that if you are the hub of a large network of people—that is, if you have a lot of connected friends or a wide social circle—you are more likely to become happy.

The same researchers are studying happiness on Facebook, which has more than 120 million active users. They've looked at who smiles in their profile pictures who doesn't, and whether their connections also smile.

James Fowler says, "We find smiling profiles cluster in much the same way as happy people cluster."

So if you want more happiness, *BE* happiness and intentionally cluster with people who smile and laugh a lot too. Doing this isn't at all selfish, because you're influencing the mass consciousness at every level.

It's not just happiness that spreads in a social network. Fowler and Christakis have also looked at trends in cigarette smoking and obesity.

The researchers showed in a New England Journal of Medicine article in May 2008 that when someone quits smoking, a friend's likelihood of quitting was 36 percent. Moreover, clusters of people who may not know one another, gave up smoking around the same time.

In a paper in the New England Journal of Medicine in July 2007 Fowler and Christakis showed that social ties also affect obesity. A person's likelihood of becoming obese increased by 57 percent if he or she had a friend who became obese.

And, like happiness, both smoking and obesity spread within three degrees of separation. Fowler says,"Beyond three, things get fuzzier."

"Eventually you get out far enough in the social network that you're competing with all these other cascades of happiness and unhappiness that are sort of duking it out."

Happiness prevails.

Pets That Find their People

Does the Oneness of Consciousness influence how dogs or cats can walk thousands of miles across country to find their human families in a place the pet has never been? There are thousands of documented cases.

Experiments prove these animals are not using scent, they're tuning into an unlimited sense of direction, an innate GPS system that uses the unified field of Consciousness.

Dogs dropped off in a strange place some distance from their homes lift their snouts high in the air and point their chest and neck in various directions. They get their bearings in three to five minutes, as though they have an internal Love compass that points them straight for home.

One story that stands out is the First World War account of Prince, an Irish Terrier devoted to his master, Private James Brown. Prince was inconsolable after his young man was posted to the battle front in France.

One day Prince disappeared from the family home in London and, to everyone's astonishment, a few weeks later ran into the arms of his James in the trenches at Armentières, France!

Since no one could believe it, Brown's commanding officer had Prince's path traced. He had made his way to the docks, befriended troops who were crossing the English Channel, and, after arriving in France, ran off to find his beloved James in the trenches. Prince became the hero of the regiment and stayed at James's side for the rest of the war.

In his book *Animal Navigation*, J.D. Carthy tells the story of two albatrosses taken from Midway Island in the Pacific and released 3,200 miles away off the coast of Washington State. One returned in ten days and the other in twelve. A third, taken to the Philippines, took a month to make the 4,000 mile journey home.

Wild species tend to hold the distance records.
Pigeons have the most amazing homing instincts,
while albatrosses, storks, terns, swallows and
starlings have all been known to find their way
home from more than a thousand miles away.

Stories of pets walking across the country to
find their beloved owners have inspired many
books and films.

One reason my dear friend Emily Andrews is so
enthusiastic about my research and speeches is
that the account of her grandmother's pets
walking from Boston to San Francisco became the
book and Disney film "Homeward Bound: The
Incredible Journey".

In his book, *Dogs That Know When Their
Owners Are Coming Home* (Three Rivers Press, 2000),
Rupert Sheldrake gives many amazing accounts
and more fully explains the energies behind the
phenomenal Consciousness skills of animals.

Sheldrake has files on hundreds of cases of
dogs reacting to a distant accident or death of a
human companion. He's documented everything
from missing dogs being found grieving at their
master's remote gravesite to a family-fed wild bird
that found the family's sick boy in a distant
hospital room.

Homing pigeons flying 3,000 miles across
America provide volumes of evidence that
awareness connected to Consciousness can see
or feel where we are in the big picture of things.

These animals with profound homing instincts
have not unplugged themselves from
Consciousness and energy sensitivities the way
humans have.

Homing instincts in wild animals, pets and
Consciousness-grounded people involve opening
the mind and heart to sensing placement in the

unified field of Consciousness and using it like a wireless global positioning system.

What a GPS system can do, *BE*ings of Consciousness can open to doing too.

Consciousness Sees

The Star Gate Project was the code name of U.S. Federal Government projects investigating phenomena of Consciousness—particularly remote viewing: the ability to see events, sites, or information from a great distance. These projects were active from the 1970s through 1995 and built upon earlier research done at The Stanford Research Institute (SRI).

Russian intelligence agencies had been spending millions developing remote viewing skills, and the CIA decided to investigate it themselves.

Under the freedom of information act 90,000 pages of top secret CIA and Department of Defense research findings were declassified and are available to the public as "The Star Gate Collection."

The preeminent physicist, Dr. Hal Puthoff, managed the CIA's projects. He used remote viewers, accomplished psychics, and proved that they could project Consciousness into highly impenetrable bunkers and accurately describe what was inside. The CIA found that superconducting shielding couldn't block it. In fact nothing could block remote viewing.

One practice incident revealed top secret information nobody on the research team knew about. They gave two remote viewers the coordinates of someone's vacation cabin in the woods of West Virginia. The cabin owner didn't know that there was a secure military installation nearby.

The two remote viewers saw the woods and the cabin, but also saw something more intriguing. Thinking that was what they were supposed to be seeing, they described a top secret underground military facility in great detail.

When the CIA checked the accuracy, the military was extremely disturbed, suspecting someone working at the site had breached security and given out highly classified information.

An investigation was launched and the matter was settled only when someone in the CIA asked the same remote viewers to search out a secret Soviet research facility of which the military had some top secret knowledge. The viewers independently created a detailed architectural sketch of an unusual crane at the site, and accurately described what was being manufactured there.

The CIA spent years developing the skills of the seven people on their remote viewing team and the results continually surprised the researchers. The remote viewers were able to predict events before they happened, including Iran's missile attack on the USS Cole and silver futures on the stock market. [1]

The renowned psychic Ingo Swan worked with the CIA's program and was able to do off-planet viewing. When he was asked to see Jupiter before the NASA fly-by, he described rings. Carl Sagan the American astronomer and astrochemist declared, "This is wrong, we know of no rings around Jupiter." Soon after that, Time magazine featured a photograph of the newly discovered thin rings around Jupiter. [2]

During the kidnapping of newspaper heiress Patty Hearst in the 1970s, the DA's office brought CIA remote viewer Pat Price to the kidnap location. He was able to accurately identify the kidnappers from police department photos, describe the kidnap vehicle and the apartment and closet she was hidden in. [3]

Remote viewers were able to create extremely accurate drawings of the underground cave Saddam Hussein, the former president of Iraq, was found hiding in. [4]

Mind Above Matter

Humans who hold the Presence of higher Consciousness in their minds tap up into the Unified Field of Consciousness where intelligence, information, experience and wisdom wait for us to connect.

We now have proof that Chinese energy practitioners of Qigong have dramatic long-distance powers. They can produce structural changes in water molecules within the stringent testing procedures of hard-nosed Western science.

After just ten minutes of Qigong energy, what we're calling Creation Consciousness, being focused on liquids like tap water, glucose, and saltwater solutions, an American-made laser spectrometer registered dramatic shifts in the spectral characteristics of liquids the Qigong masters had never touched. [5]

Some of the experiments were conducted by renowned Qigong Master and healer Yan Xin from a distance of nearly 2000 kilometers. [6]

Consciousness Influences Water

Studies of salted water being influenced by the focused Consciousness of healers show shifts in oxygen-hydrogen bonds—as if magnets were being used. Russian research on psychokinesis shows changes in crystalline structure—again an influencing of water's oxygen-hydrogen bonds.

Our thoughts and intentions change molecular structures outside ourselves.

Dr. Masaru Emoto, a Japanese quantum physicist wondered: What is the quantum physics of a snowflake? Why are they not the same, what's going on, how does this happen?

His questions led him to undertake experiments that showed what we think and focus upon can affect the molecular structure of water without us ever touching that water. Interest in his work has spread around the world, and he's written six New York Times best-selling books on the subject.

When a Buddhist monk focused Consciousness into water with thoughts like Love and Gratitude, the molecular organization of the water was altered, creating magnificent snowflakes when the water was frozen. Thoughts like "you fool" reduced the molecular structure to just mush. These experiments have been duplicated around the world.

Your body is up to 75% water being influenced, reformed and energized by your thoughts, emotions and higher Consciousness. Dr. Emoto's beautiful book *The Healing Power of Water* illustrates how powerfully your thoughts and beliefs—what and how you are *being*—affect the new cells you are constantly creating.

Dr. Konstantin Korotkov confirms that now we have absolutely clear scientific evidence of water absorbing and holding information.

"Chemicals, technology and human intention all influence water," says Dr. Korotkov.

"If we have good, purely structured water it is tremendously positive for our bodies. If this water is charged with electromagnetic fields or negative human emotions it can totally destroy human health. This has been proven.

"The evidence suggests that about 40% of human health problems come from bad water."

The Memory of Water

Water is the essential mover and communicator of all Life processes—the perfect transport medium for nutrients, blood cells, and enzymes in the body. It "memorizes" and carries energy forward. French government scientist Jacques Benveniste surprised the scientific community in the 1980s by announcing he had discovered the "memory of water." Using a series of electromagnetic coils wrapped around metal containers, Benveniste transferred "information" from a flask of poison into a flask of water.

When the *poisonized* water was placed on bacteria, the bacteria promptly died—as if it had been exposed to the original poison. The water had "copied" the chemical's potentials, though not a single molecule of the poison was in the water. [7]

Water absorbs the Consciousness of other presences to which it is exposed.

German physicist Dr Wolfgang Ludwig has proven that even purified water still contains the electromagnetic frequencies of toxic contaminants to which it was previously exposed.

He also confirms that these lingering unwanted signals can destroy health. Dr. Luwig says, "Water has the ability to transfer information, once it has obtained it, to other systems such as living organisms". He's also proven you can "erase" this information. [8]

A device invented by Austrian Johann Grander restructured water by passing it alongside chambers of sealed "healthy information" water. The water goes through a "revitalization," and German environmental water expert Dr Horst Felsch was surprised to determine this bottled 'Grander water' could "keep virtually forever"— without the use of chemical preservatives.

This chemical-free process is used to reduce bacteria counts in many municipal swimming pools in Europe.

Italian physicists at the University of Milan discovered that, unlike any other liquid, water behaves like a laser as it transfers electromagnetic frequencies through a resonance between water molecules. [9]

This explains a mystery that has long baffled biologists: how cells communicate through living organisms in near-instantaneous physiological reactions to emotions such as fear and anger.

All of everything on Earth is absorbing humanity's mass Consciousness values and behaviors.

Humanity, terrorized and afraid of itself, is destroying Life itself.

Discoveries in the mathematics field known as *dynamics*, show us that the end points toward which systems point themselves are supported, reinforced and determined by changes in morphogenic fields. We are morphing the BEingness of everything!

The Oneness of everything is absorbing our collective Consciousness, including a collective militaristic doomsday death wish. The good-old-boy greed-fueled, mechanistic militarism is the cancerous heart of big business and big government piracy that's been stealing not just money, it's been pirating the possibility for Life on Earth!

For Life to survive, unconscious business and government must be allowed to implode into the black holes of their own greed. It's high time!

Biologists around the world are reporting dramatic decreases in birth rates in countless species.

This is our wake-up call!

Humanity's mainstream values, agendas, purposes, goals, and intentions are morphing the future on every level of energy—from the purity of water, the bloodstream of all Life, to the chaotic energy we're putting into the atmosphere through industrial and emotional pollutants of every kind.

The mass Consciousness of humanity is co-creating or co-destroying Life, so Love Loving Life with your values, choices, purchases and actions!

Collective Consciousness

Consciousness is carried forward through time into the collective awareness of subsequent generations.

In the early 1900s, when barbed wire was first introduced to fence in livestock, there was hardly a horse that wasn't scarred by it. But within fifty years both cattle and horses were born knowing how to avoid injury. A whole species had gathered an instinctive Consciousness.

Something similar happened with cattle guards—
a series of parallel steel pipes laid between gate
posts to eliminate the need for gates. Because
they're spaced over a pit, a rancher's trucks can
drive over them, but animal hooves immediately
drop into the hole beneath. The first generations
of livestock learned the hard way that trying to
walk over them was dangerous and painful, but
present-day cattle are born knowing this, and they
don't even try to cross them. Now ranchers
throughout the west save money by just painting
stripes with the same spacing and color as the
pipes.

Herds never exposed to real cattle guards don't
cross them because the knowing in the collective
Consciousness has been added to their field
of instinct.

Experiments by a highly skeptical researcher,
Steven Rose, at the Open University in England,
indicated that even behaviors of day-old chicks
can be influenced by the experiences of their day-
old predecessors. Subsequent batches of chicks
hatched already knowing to avoid pecking at a
yellow light that had negative associations. [10]

In the 1980s, military intelligence studies by
James Flynn indicated a gradual and predictable
increase in performance on I.Q. tests in twenty
countries. I.Q. scores began their three-percent
rise per decade before the invention of television,
and they continue this gradual climb. Researchers
conclude that intelligence follows mass
Consciousness too. [11]

We are in a morphing field of Oneness, and the
higher we rise through Consciousness, the more
intuition, instinct, knowing, ability, wisdom,
connection, and Oneness we ALL share.

The extrasensory awareness most humans have maintained is the sense that someone is looking at us from behind, because throughout our embattled centuries, attackers have tended to sneak up from behind.

There are greater abilities and survival instincts we need to open ourselves to being. During the great Earth changes that increase and intensify crises of weather and Nature, we'll need them to survive.

A mind open to being Consciousness connects us like a wireless laptop computer accessing information and intelligence through the atmosphere. Being one with higher Consciousness greatly enhances all levels of well-being.

Rational Proof of Oneness

Biologist and Consciousness researcher Rupert Sheldrake has investigated animal abilities to predict oncoming seizures in people as well as big scale events such as earthquakes and tsunamis. During the Indonesian tsunami of 2004, doomed tourists gathered shells on the beach, while every species of animal, from birds to mice and rats, headed to higher ground.

These animals had never experienced such an event before, but every species instinctively knew where to go.

The animal kingdom has a sophisticated, instantaneous communication system that only Consciousness delivers.

Have you ever known a pet that would anticipate the arrival of a family member?

Sheldrake discovered that 60% of dogs and 50% of the cats in a Los Angeles study anticipated the return home of at least one family member—regardless of the time of day, distance involved, or manner of travel. Other cities surveyed were London, Ramsbottom (in northwest England), and Santa Cruz, California. On average 50% of dogs and 30% of cats anticipate the return of their owners. The highest incidences are among the toy and non-sporting dogs.

His research revealed that anticipation starts the very moment the owners make the decision to come home. Sheldrake placed a video camera inside the front door of each home and a video camera on the dog's owner—both with time codes so the time would be precisely tracked.

When owners were not on their way home, dogs would spend only 4% of the time by the door. However, at the very moment their owners thought of being home, 86% of the dogs began behaving in ways that showed active anticipation of their humans' arrival.

The key moment was when the owner thought about being home. This happened even with skeptical owners.

While cats do not wait by the front door as often as dogs do, they are able to know in advance when their owners are planning to take them to the veterinarian. Sheldrake contacted veterinary offices near where he lives in London to find out if they had observed any problem with cat owners keeping their appointments. Not only had all 65 offices noticed such problems, some were no longer making appointments for cat owners. Their explanation is "Cat appointments don't work."

Before there were any visible signs or movements, cats would frantically hide because they sensed their owners' intention to take them to the vet!

Many cats only react to a ringing phone when their owners are calling home. Some families say their cats lift the receivers and meow to their beloved owners even when they're phoning home from across the world.

Cats have another interesting talent—they often seem able to inspire their humans to open the door at precisely the moment the cat is ready to walk through it.

Sheldrake believes that human abilities to use the field of Consciousness have atrophied.

The Oneness of Consciousness

It was Arthur C. Clarke, coauthor of the film "2001: A Space Odyssey," who correctly said highly-advanced technology is essentially indistinguishable from magic.

Again and again, research is proving that one person's focused Consciousness affects the environment as well as in another person's brainwaves.

Princeton Engineering's Anomalies Research Center measures group quantum super-radiance. Their random Event Generator (REG) machines are like social thermometers, sensing delicate disturbances to the field of Consciousness when an event impacts many people. [12]

Around the world these devices registered our response to 9/11 and to the death of Princess Diana. However, there was one event that was anticipated down to the moment it was going to happen: people had time to collect around radios and televisions when the verdict was read in the O.J. Simpson trial.

Millions of people had a visceral attachment to what the outcome would say about race, wealth, and the law. The moment of the verdict created an enormous peaking never seen before.

That shiver through the collective spine spiked the Consciousness readers at Princeton, the University of Nevada, and the University of Amsterdam. The odds of this being a fluke are greater than 1,000 to one.

The mass Consciousness is like air and water, a disturbance creates a wave that expands throughout the world.

Several scientists including Einstein and Stephen Hawking have estimated that a shift in the Consciousness of only 75,000 to 100,000 people, changes the mass Consciousness of the planet.

Entrainment

Creation Consciousness synchronizes and harmonizes interactions that travel through space. I was stunned the day I personally witnessed this.

I walked into the San Francisco garage of a very old collector and repairer of pendulum clocks. There were thirty antique pendulum clocks on various shelves, all ticking and tocking in perfect unison. Amazed, I asked, "How do you get them all to swing in unison?"

I assumed he had a person holding each pendulum release at the same moment, so the clock cacophony wouldn't drive him mad.

The old gentlemen didn't even look up from his work, as he said matter of factly, "They do it themselves."

I was highly doubtful.

"I'm not the first person to ask that question am I?"

"You're the first to ask in the past ten minutes!" he said, still not looking up from his tinkering.

Christiaan Huygens, a notable physicist, coined the term "entrainment" in 1666 after he noticed that two pendulum clocks had moved into the same swinging rhythm, and subsequent experiments duplicated this process.

Amazingly, the tick and tock synchronize even though the lengths of the pendulums are different and create a different rate of phase.

Physicists explain that small amounts of energy are transferred between the two systems when they are out of phase in such a way as to produce non-resonance or negative feedback. As the clocks communicate through the air, they create a more harmonious phase.

For reasons that baffle conventional medicine, the menstruation cycles of women who live closely together will synchronize.

Creation harmonizes.

The human brain tends to synchronize its dominant EEG frequency with external stimuli. Our brainwaves are always entraining with the sounds around us.

Entrainment is deliberately used to control our pace within a society. The rapid-fire imagery of television, advertising, and music, and the rushed rhythm of a busy city are always entraining us to pick up the pace of the human race—a frenzied race to what finish line?

Living at the speed of Life is something else completely. Listening to waves on a shore, peacefully absorbing the rhythms of crickets at night, the slow crackling of a camp fire—these are all ways we re-mind ourselves to relax and entrain with Creation.

Entrained People

Several studies done since 1963 prove
Consciousness entrains. Research by Rollin
McCraty of the Institute of HeartMath shows that
when two simpatico people touch, the heart
rhythm of one can entrain the brain of the other. [13]

Scientists at the University of Freiburg in
Germany proved that we don't even have to be
close to one another to share a common mind.
Their research placed two people—one sending
thoughts, intention or experience, and the other
person being mentally open to receiving—in
different shielded rooms. The EEG of the distant
receiver gradually showed the same brainwave
patterns and responses to stimulation as the
sender. Some receivers showed instantaneous
responses to a light being flashed in the eyes of
the senders. The two were entrained. [14]

The results were repeated with similar research
in Mexico and The U.S. [15]

However, there is a condition for us to connect
with the Oneness of mind.

Investigators from both Seattle's Bastyr
University and the University of Washington
concur that entrainment happens only between
people who'd "bonded" by spending 20 minutes
with each other in meditative silence. In every one
of these studies, experience had become
entwined; the recipients were "seeing" or feeling
what their partners actually saw or felt in real
time, only after shared meditation.

Aka Threads

Hawaiian and some South American cultures called entrainment "aka threads." Their highest form of artistic expression was the weaving of tapestries. These cultures believed that after two people make a heart connection, a thread of energy forever exists between them. They believed we're all weaving the great tapestry of Creation with the aka threads we create with one another.

How often have you had someone say, "I was just thinking of you, and here you are!"

You've tugged the heart string of an aka thread sometimes from the other side of the world.

Being expanding Consciousness opens you to greater and greater aspects of Oneness, and science is beginning to understand why.

Once the quantum particles of Consciousness connect, science is proving that their "relationship" lasts and lasts. There is an ongoing, instantaneous dialogue that is the symphony of being.

The threads of caring, the entanglement between human Consciousness and Creation's Consciousness, is weaving and becoming a multidimensional tapestry that is our Universe.

We are Life's co-architects.

Now the great enlightenment of Oneness is dawning. The dark ages of tyrannical greed are collapsing and fading to lightness, as we usher in Our Renaissance of Consciousness.

CHAPTER 3

We Are
Co-creators

Scientific breakthroughs prove atmospheric energies respond to heartfelt beliefs. Our inner experience creates outer reality more powerfully than we've been taught to believe.

Energetically, you are a container, a receiver and a broadcaster, and what you put out into the world you will get back.

Chaos creates chaos
Consciousness creates Life.

A Consciousness of Place

Do families *"live into"* a home so its atmosphere is in synch with its people? Does an inventor's intensely desired outcome empower the creation zone? Do artists really *"condition"* a new studio's environment?

The answer is yes.

Science is proving that human Consciousness co-mingles to create the energy of a place.

Former Princeton Engineering Anomaly Research (PEAR) scientist Dr Roger Nelson compared several sites such as Wounded Knee in the US and the Queen's Chamber in the Great Pyramid of Egypt. He used a random-event generator (REG), the electronic device that registers changes in the randomness of the Zero Point Field (the ocean of microscopic vibrations, energy, information, and Consciousness in the space between things).

He discovered each of these historically important places maintain a uniquely charged environment. [1]

A phenomenon well-known to inventors is the "garage-inventor effect." Inventors are often able to gradually produce spectacular results in their own garage or laboratory; however, the results are not repeatable anywhere else.

The extraordinary studies of Dr. William A. Tiller, former physics professor emeritus at Stanford University, proved our conscious intentions are unique energies that can be captured and used at a future time to affect a living system.

In a study published in The Journal of Scientific Exploration, Tiller had a group of meditators "charge" IIED boxes, (intentional imprinted electrical devices) with intentions which were recorded and replayed at different labs up to 2,000 miles away.

The experimenters discovered boxed intentions would produce desired effects including increasing enzyme activity, speeding up the development of fruit flies, changing the pH of a solution, and even changing water and air temperatures.

They also found that they were "conditioning the space" in the labs. If the studies went on for more than three months, the energies unique to that environment manifested greater results, increasing up to 100 times. In other words, the labs became energetically intensified environments for this experiment.

The researchers also discovered profound changes in the ambient Zero Point Field of the labs. The ordinary fluctuations of the quantum field were being uniquely reorganized. The human intentions had a lasting effect!

Multiple test sites showed strong similarities.

Tiller observed a similar human *charging* of space, a unique "super-symmetry", at sites along the meridian system of the human body. These meridian points (often called *chakras*) defy conventional physics by maintaining a highly unusual and refined energy. [2]

This concentrated Consciousness breaks the rules of conventional physics by having an exotic super-symmetry where both electric and magnetic dipoles coexist and function.

So, what does this all mean?

Consciousness is a realm of energy not affected by polarity, the way other Earthly energy is.

Tiller's experiments indicate that our values, beliefs, thoughts, and choices alter our bodies and the environment in lasting ways—as if the planet's atmosphere and all living systems within it are being programmed with Life, by Life. We're constantly co-writing the Life code. Human agendas are viral; spreading copies of themselves out to either enhance or harm our delicate, living biosphere.

What Dr. William Tiller's "black box" experiments prove is that thoughts transverse time and space and have a tendency to cling to one another and reinforce themselves. When we're thinking the same thought in a group, the power of the thought compounds—and these thoughts influence the order of things regardless of physical distance.

This is why it's important to realize that if we're believing everything is all getting worse and out of control...then it will, from our inner *being* and Life out to the planet.

To *be* the change, to *be* creatively and resourcefully alive, Love Loving Life however it is now.

The Mind of Mass Consciousness

Over a span of more than twenty years, the Transcendental Meditation organization systematically determined that group mind reduces violence and discord in the world. Dozens and dozens of experiments produced definitive data, and the studies were published in impressive peer-reviewed journals such as "The Journal of Mind and Behavior" and "Social Indicators Research." [3]

In 1993, a two-month study gathered 4,000 people in Washington D.C. for daily meditations on peacefulness and harmony to determine the influence of "group calm" on the broader community.

Violent crime, which had been steadily increasing during the first five months of the year, began to drop and continued to drop until the end of the experiment.

As soon as the group of 4,000 people disbanded, the crime rate rose again. The group reduced violent crime by 86 percent. A similar effect was proven in 24 other U.S. cities. [4]

Each of the studies on crime considered variables such as changes in population, college population, population density, percentage of young people, ratio of police to population, and neighborhood watch projects.

Whenever just one percent of the population was practicing regular TM, the crime rate dropped to 24 percent of the previous average. These findings were published in peer-reviewed journals that accept only solid research and science.

Ten years earlier, in a 1983 study of a special TM assembly in Israel, the Arab-Israeli conflict was tracked over a two-month period.

The number of meditators had a direct correlation on war deaths in Lebanon. When the number of meditators was high, war deaths consistently fell by 76 per cent, and local crime, traffic accidents, and fires also decreased. [5] These studies all considered outside factors—such as weather, weekends, and holidays—which might skew results.

Similar experiments were repeated in the Netherlands over a 10-year period. Groups of people with enhanced Consciousness focused on peacefulness that would lower crime and traffic accidents. On every occasion, the Dutch Central Office for Statistics confirmed a significant drop in crime and traffic accidents. [6]

Mass Consciousness creates community and quality of Life, however as long as the media intensifies fear and broadcasts values that create violence and crime, we're losing Consciousness to a soul-sucking black hole within the lowest common denominators.

Intelligence and Consciousness will continue to migrate, to learn from trusted awareness and wisdom flowing through the Internet.

Influencing mass Consciousness is like singing or chanting: the more people participate in unison, the greater the vibrational effect.

But how many people are needed for an intention to have a positive impact?

According to the Transcendental Meditation organization, it takes the square root of one per cent of a population—approximately 1600 people to have a positive impact on the USA. To globally influence the world, they say about 70,000 people would be a good start.

British theoretical physicist Stephen Hawking agrees, saying global mass Consciousness is influenced by 78,000 people. That's a fraction of the audience for an evening newscast or one violent, dumbed down, film.

You vote, and co-create our future, with every purchase.

Every time you watch a program, you're the one being programmed! Every time you buy a product you're co-creating social values, the mass Consciousness and our quality of Life! You license corporations to keep on doing what they've been doing.

Imagine if we transformed the terrorizing tactics that oppressive governments and alarmist media put out into our world. Imagine if we decided to turn off the toxicity broadcast into our homes and hearts and actively let those who produce it know we're on a toxicity fast.

The mass Consciousness and the fear-mongering media would quickly lift themselves up and be energy multipliers of Life's solutions rather than it's problem.

Two Minute Healing
Imagine All The People

Feel how beautiful it would feel to awaken morning after beautiful blue-skied morning, knowing you're living in a world that Loves Loving Life!

Imagine mothers and fathers purchasing only products of higher Consciousness. Those products will become mainstream, more affordable, and entire industries will clean up their presence.

Focusing on what you're *against* is not creative, but energizing what you are *for,* and recommending it, empowers excellence. It inspires the less conscious to awaken and join The Renaissance of Consciousness. Shoppers quickly send messages of changing awareness, values and Consciousness to corporations and retailers. By supporting conscious commerce, in less than one year, we'll rejuvenate our economy in sustainable ways. Imagine entire stores choosing to feature products of higher Consciousness.

Imagine consumer confidence being rejuvenated by consumer Consciousness.

Imagine that. Feel how that future will feel.

Experience what that will feel like: masses of shoppers quietly and calmly cleaning up industry at the checkout counters of the stores. Imagine local conscious commerce hiring people and treating them well, and economies and Nature coming back to health.

Experience how it will feel to awaken day after day to a healthier, more hopeful and peacefully healed world. Feel how beautiful that feels.

Open your mind and your heart and allow that future into your beliefs. Give it the Light of hope, and you're on your way to activating and co-creating solutions.

Awakenings of Co-Creation

The scientific pioneers and innovative champions of conscious commerce I've cited in these first three chapters inspire us to open our hearts and minds to the possibilities of new paradigms.

Science, with its limiting double-blind studies can't equal a human being's ability to sense and *be* higher Consciousness and oneness with ALL.

We are the ultimate instruments and co-creators of Consciousness, so the leap of faith we must each take is to trust what we intimately experience as real and worthy. At times the lightness of *being* higher Consciousness is magnificent, divine and beyond words.

Grow the expansive magnificence of Loving Life. Trust the heartwarming blissful enlightenment.

Bliss with *being* is expansive Consciousness co-creating Life.

The following chapters offer you access to the joy-expanding realm of Consciousness. Take a magic carpet ride without leaving your chair.

CHAPTER 4
Creation Consciousness

So are you convinced that we're part of the orchestrating architectural Consciousness creating and sustaining Life on Earth?

In the live "Conscious Cabarets" I'm doing now, the following information really opens hearts and minds.

The cosmic recipe for a planet that creates and sustains complex Life involves a tremendous number of ingredients, factors, temperatures and elements.

All of these ingredients must be interactive, checked, balanced and sustained for Life to happen in this moment as this moment.

If our planet were only 5% closer to our Sun, complex life forms would perish because of a runaway greenhouse effect. Our home is orbiting in a very narrow band of space that scientists call "The Goldilocks Zone." Not too hot. Not too cold.

What follows are some of the Cosmic essentials for you to be reading these words now.

★ a host planet orbiting a dwarf star not too large or small, too cool or hot.

★ a planet with a moderate rate of rotation

★ a planet protected by other gas giant planets.

★ a planet in a nearly circular orbit.

★ an oxygen rich atmosphere.

★ a planet having the correct mass to support life.

★ a moon large enough to stabilize the planet's orbit.

★ a consistent magnetic gravitational field.

★ a planet with enough interior heat to maintain its liquid iron core, generate a gravitational and magnetic field and comfortably warm the surface.
★ a delicate ratio of liquid water and continents to sustain a life-supporting biosphere.
★ a terrestrial planet with a crust having the perfect thickness to maintain constant plate tectonic activity.

This list could go on and on.

If our Sun were larger, stronger, weaker, or smaller, we would not be here.

If our planet were smaller, its magnetic field would be weak and allow solar winds to strip away our atmosphere, leaving Earth as barren as Mars.

Our Earth's atmosphere is a thin blue ribbon of Life and light. It is 78% nitrogen, 21% oxygen and 1% carbon dioxide. This delicate recipe assures us a temperate climate, protection from solar radiation and the delicious combination of gasses necessary for liquid water and millions of interdependent species of complex Life.

The film "The Privileged Planet" (Illustra Media) is based on Guillermo Gonzalez's book *The Privileged Planet: How Our Place in the Cosmos Is Designed for Discovery* (Regnery Publishing, 2004). Gonzalez shows us the astounding miracle of Creation that we are. The astronomers he interviewed have conservatively estimated the probability of attaining the ingredients of Life on Earth simultaneously.

The likelihood that your Life in this moment is a random fluke is assigned the number 1, compared the the likelihood that there is intelligent, Consciousness orchestrating ongoing Life. It looks like this.

$$\frac{1}{1,000,000,000,000,000}$$

The odds that our Life on Earth is a randomly arranged fluke of dumb interrelating energies is one thousandth of one trillion.

When we add to this longest of all long shots your conscious intelligence, your ability to contemplate what you're contemplating now, we've gone beyond all comprehensible odds.

Reality, evidence and likelihood vastly favor the omnipresence of an architectural Consciousness guiding Life's Creation in this moment as this moment.

It hardly seems possible that anyone who refuses to believe in an intelligent Consciousness of Creation will have read this far. However, in the event it is required course reading and you identify with the fluke, then just Love the fluke!

If there is anything of Life that you Love, then Love Loving *the fluke* that delivered you to it! That will lift you higher!

Now back to the rest of us.

Open Your Love

Consciousness is the single largest component of our Universe and when we study it we see that its wondrous agenda throughout our solar system is to smoothly, creatively and abundantly create more Consciousness through Life on Earth.

Our entire solar system is maintaining Earth's presence, in this moment, for your Life to be happening.

Opening your heart and mind to this is transformational.

Take a moment to think of what you Love about your Life.

Allow your gratitude for *being* to open your heart and expand to fill you.

Open your mind like a blossom and feel gratitude for your Life on Earth.
Love Loving Life for a few moments now.

Love Loving ALL of Life just as it is now and you'll experience a profound release and peace with ALL. This lifts you up.

Polarity Rules Unconsciousness

When we have unconscious minds closed tight as a box, a nation's people can be convinced there are two sides to everything—and that Creation prefers *us* to *them*. We'll unconsciously follow an invading regime straight into the greed-fueled Hell that is war, so dumbed down we'll believe chaos creates peace.

It never does.

Every war or fight ends with communication, humility and diplomacy; the Consciousness that creates peace.

Politics polarizes.

polarize | ˈpōləˌrīz | verb

To divide or cause to divide into two sharply contrasting groups or sets of opinions or beliefs.

The essence of humanity and ALL Life is beyond the pulls of polarity. Consciousness transcends polarity.

The pure essence of higher Consciousness wants Life to be simply, Lovingly beautiful.

It's greed that complicates things.

Being higher Consciousness unifies us and lasting solutions are co-created for whatever issues we've been battling.

Far more creative than just the laws of intention or attraction, being higher Consciousness connects you with the realm of energy that orchestrates everything.

When the ego's competitions, comparisons and addictions are collapsed, being Consciousness co-creates with all the energies around you.

There is nothing more creatively empowered than higher Consciousness delivering sustainable solutions.

Follow Good Energy

Living as higher Consciousness lifts and attunes you to higher,more connective and creative stratas of energies. It lifts you above the dream that became a nightmare: the trappings of comparative, competitive success, a quicksand culture of human doings, human wantings, and humans' addictive hyper-having. It liberates you from greed.

In a moment of enlightenment, Consciousness collapses the fearful ego, liberates the mind and we're outside the box—where Life flows! It is there we experience our Oneness with Oneness!

Concepts and issues are centered in beliefs—mental attachments—that don't have sides. Despite what we've been carefully taught, even the issues and concepts political and social leaders leverage to devise our divisiveness don't have sides. They merely have sources, realities and solutions. Most often an open mind and Life-Loving heart are the solution.

What we're calling Consciousness is the only energy of our planet that is not affected by the magnetic pull of the poles. It is of a higher energy realm than gravity and polarization.

The sooner we liberate ourselves from polarizing low-Consciousness, from being one-sided, the sooner Creation's Consciousness will flow through each of us, through our mass Consciousness and our social and business agendas.

Clinging to one side of an issue is to be mired and lost in an illusion.

We need only to reflect on humanity's history of fear and racism to realize that the solution to conflict is opening minds and hearts to Oneness.

Mother Earth's pneumonia is bringing this lesson home. Wherever you may be, we're all here together as this one Life plan.

Peace and rejuvenation are
not team sports.
Peace is BEing Oneness with ALL.
Rejuvenation requires higher
Consciousness.

Architecture of Apocalypse

Humanity has been deliberately and strategically unplugged from Oneness for more than six centuries.

Between the 13th-17th centuries greed in the form of land ownership, social hierarchies, feudalism, slavery, and the crusading of fear-fueled divisive religiosity strangled the Oneness of higher Consciousness out of us.

Descartes

René Descartes' book of *Principia philosophiae* (Principles of Philosophy) 1644 featured numerous incorrect assumptions. Some of these were good for the business of making people conquerers of the Earth, so the aristocracy published and enforced them and they remain foundational beliefs still taught by westernized schools and religions.

Descartes stated that bodies can act on each other only through contact.

This lie is Life's cancer.

The teaching that everything is separate has been fostered by governments, armies and religions for centuries.

As long as we feel alienated from Creation, enslaved by choking debts and the struggle to fulfill our lives through politicized institutions, we are bickering, empty, weak, addictive and unconscious to what's really happening. And that's exactly what greed-addicted aristocracies have always needed slaves to be.

Newton

In 1687 Isaac Newton published *Philosophiæ Naturalis Principia Mathematica* (Mathematical Principles of Natural Philosophy). During the dark ages of Consciousness it was considered one of the most important scientific works ever written.

Newton's laws of motion were used to convince humanity that our world operates through classical mechanics. He established so many different laws of the natural world with such economy, that his tenets and methods still form the rigid beliefs most scientists and doctors cling to almost three and a half centuries later.

New science has proven these theories to be wrong. Life, the planet and Consciousness are not mechanical.

There is great resistance to these truths because to embrace them requires the scrapping of many old-school paradigms, beliefs, agendas and rules. The breakthroughs of Conscious Science invite great awakenings and change, so the old school of mechanizing and militarizing will have none of it, even when it is proven time after time using their own rules.

Aristocracies strategically groomed the science and philosophies of Descartes and Newton for publication and education. They popularized philosophies of isolated mechanics to crush our Consciousness of Oneness. They kept their soldiers and slaves performing like ashamed, terrorized, isolated machines.

They've historically used the shock and awe of warfare to massacre the young, smart and strong, to maintain fear and keep the masses taxed and tithing to the aristocratic wizards of these self-dooming Ozs.

Before these dark ages, most cultures related to Creation and the planet as one, alive, organic Presence of Creation's light!

Unpoliticized people lived pastoral lives as the opening, enlightening Presence of Creation in the moment, PURELY AS THE MOMENT!

Minds and hearts were open so the living spirit of Creation, Creation's pure orchestrating Presence flowed through us as us.

Try living Life at the speed of Life, rather than the speed of money.

How Holocaust and Apocalypse Happen

We cannot fully alienate ourselves from Creation's Consciousness because it is omnipresent. However, we can tune Consciousness out, let fear close our minds and hearts and sell our collective soul to what we've been carefully taught is most mighty.

It happened in pre-World War II Germany and it's happening again. To more fully understand this see the documentary film "Thrive".

Unconsciousness spreads chaos through every level of being. As social and economic tyranny and wars rage on, we all become soldiers of misfortune, feeling miserably embattled, lost to our Life's potentials, heart's wisdom, and the simple benevolences of being the harmony of Oneness.

When we relate to everything through brands and economic one-sidedness we're left without a clue as to how anything actually *IS*.

We're disconnected, living in a parallel reality, feeling lost, needy, confused and dependent on the interpretations and guidance of those who seek to control us through fear.

Shock doctrines are formulas used by invading entities to create the illusion of enemies and crisis. They strategically leverage fear and chaos to empower an aristocracy so that, during the shock and awe, they can shift influence, wealth and resources to big business and the military-industrial complex. [2]

Evil dwells where Consciousness is shadowed by greed and fear.

The truth is Oneness, and every photo of our one round planet whirling through space proves it.

Our Community of Consciousness realizes that we don't need to own or control something to Love experiencing it. In fact ownership and controlling smother the breath of pure experience.

In the aftermath of war, communal living, skills, trade, barter, co-ops, and generosity of spirit open new avenues of trade and commerce that liberate us to exchange real commodities and services, without playing the money game. As I write this barter is experiencing a boom.

Many people in the Community of Consciousness are heading for the hills, returning to the earth, homesteading off the grid, planting, growing, harvesting with a cooperative Consciousness of bounty.

We who
Live to Love
ALL of Life
become bliss.

Two Minute Healing

Healing Alien-Nations

Together let's share a long deep cleansing breath of our one Biosphere. We are breathing oxygen from our forests and the moisture from our oceans. Without them, this Life we share could not exist. Feel the Life-giving plan and its energy surrounding, filling and fueling you in this and every moment.

Open your mind and your heart and feel yourself on this stunningly beautiful planet, this one, beautiful, round garden of Life.

When we pull our view way back and see our blue, green and alive planet in the vastness of space, we realize that our whole planet is the garden of eden.

This whole planet is our Cosmic garden of Eden.

Feel that energy in your heart. Open your heart and let it glow and shine. Let hardness, regret and fear melt away, and let your heart's light shine.

Love Loving this miracle Life!

Feel yourself present on the beautiful planet that gives you Life in this moment. Feel yourself surrounded by Creation's Love of Life.

Open your gratitude.

And open your awareness and *BE* the Oneness of Life now.

Love Loving Life! Bathe the whole world in this, your heart's gratitude for *being*.

CHAPTER 5

The Open Mind

A computer does nothing without the electricity that activates its programs and memory. A brain does nothing without the electricity that is the mind.

The mind is refined electrical activation in and around the brain. Researchers have discovered that much of the mind's activities are happening *around* the brain, outside the skull. These findings are truly blowing our minds right out of the closed box within which we've been so carefully taught to exist.

Imagine a satellite dish folded in on itself. How much information could be taken in or transmitted out?

Almost none.

Thinking outside the box requires a mind's energy field to be open, so information can move in and out.

At this moment, your mind and body, the walls of buildings, and everything in your environment are infiltrated with vast amounts of electromagnetic fields and messages.

Cell phone calls compounded with radio and television signals and satellite transmissions are penetrating every fiber of everything around you. We tap into these signals only when we have an open, powered-up electronic device attuned to receive.

It's the same with the human mind.

Dr. Carl Pribram, the eminent neurosurgeon, says, "We've been corrupted for a century by things and statistics." [1]

In earlier millennia, little of what is in this book would be surprising to people because they lived as energy interacting with energy. They lived as Consciousness opening to Oneness with Creation's Consciousness, the architecturally, orchestrating Presence of ALL.

Without higher Consciousness our minds are unplugged from Creation's delicate balances, logic and reason; and our hearts and minds become toxic life-sucking black holes of ego, fear, darkness, cruelty, and greed-addicted destruction.

If this sounds like just another day at work it sheds some enlightenment on why people can be so selfishly evil, make destructive choices and do such hurtful things. What we've been taught is an egoic power hungry personality called the Devil, is simply the chaos that happens when people's energy is cut off from the Light of Creation's Consciousness and drops down into heavy, low, dark vibrational realms. At these levels the fabric of our dimension frays.

In recent centuries we were carefully taught to relate to Creation and chaos as if they have flawed personalities, competing agendas and petty human emotions.

Only an outsider vying for influence and control would teach a child to fear their parent. So, why have we been taught to have a fear-centered relationship with Life's ongoing Creation?

Because fear alienates, handicaps and confuses, it unplugs us from our source and weakens us as it empowers the agents of the fear.

Fear weakened people, seeking social approval, can be convinced to turn weapons on innocent citizens of their own nation, for the glory of an ideology or regime.

The realms of higher Consciousness that create Now, that patiently and silently create you and everything of this moment, are above and beyond petty, competitive, polarizing agendas.

Presence is Consciousness, an energy realm that transcends polarity and pettiness. It opens to us through pure energies that transcend words.

Without the unconsciousness

of addictive greed,

there is peace and sustainable

prosperity.

This is why the change, the shift, must happen within ALL of us.

Know-it-alls are often described as "close-minded" or "thick-headed" because they have a closed-box mind with thick, protective walls.

Their minds are made up and have become more like windowless bunkers than opening blossoms.

A healthy mind has the shape of an open lotus blossom. A healthy mind is a fully opened satellite dish, receiving and broadcasting.

The akashic records are in the intelligence of our atmosphere. Our watery biosphere records information and the akasha is all around you now.

As Earth changes happen, a high Consciousness mind open to instinct, extrasensory abilities and uncommon common sense will be standard equipment for survival.

If you have not opened and

changed your mind today,

you have not learned

and have not fully absorbed or

reflected what Life is now.

Two Minute Healing

Open Your Mind

The latin root of the word inspiration is "inspirare"—to breathe in.

Feel the energy in and around your brain. Intensify that energy, as if you have an internal dimmer switch. Turn up the energy and feel the shape of your mind.

Does it feel open—or closed and contained?

Open it—like a great blossom opening out.

Open it until it has the expansive shape of a broad, open, energy satellite dish that can receive and send information.

Let your mind's energy enlighten and expand out. Feel the weight of containment, the weight of a heavy mind lift off you.

Open, relax, so Consciousness, Life source and our atmosphere may breathe through your mind.

Allow your mind to be open, to receive, to be Oneness, and feel the beautiful lightness of simply being.

Allow your mind to stay open, calm and able to receive inspiration, solutions and creativity.

In the future, whenever you feel pressure on your mind, allow it to open, relax, and let Life in.

Instant Gratification

Instant gratification lacks depth. Too much too soon is too shallow.

A closed, high-pressure mind demands constant distraction from its pain. Sex, drugs, alcohol and rock and roll are at the ready to numb that pain.

The more we become addicted to needing more and bigger thrills, the more we buy into the lie that internal well-being is the product of the external, merchandizing parallel reality. If we buy into that lie, we've been convinced, in order to feel, we must buy and have.

When a whole nation is addicted, the status of stuff is the high. When we're all snorting at the cocaine bowl of money and no one is Consciousness of when or how to stop, history has seen collapse time after time.

Borrowing billions of dollars to rescue unconscious, greed-addicted bankers is like giving addicts a cocaine party, and then expecting them to choose sobriety.

Ancient ruins are the relics of entire cultures and civilizations collapsed into the black hole of greed- driven immediate gratifications.

Higher Consciousness
is the sweet reward
of higher Consciousness.

Soul Thievery

We've had higher Consciousness alienated from our beings. Our authentic essence was stolen so we'd be masses of human doings, human wantings, human havings and human gettings, rather than humans *BE*ing.

Low Consciousness institutions masterfully imprint our brains. Their deliberate strategy has been to create generations of poorly educated, isolated individuals who lack logic and reason.

The Westernized way has been to create sensation-addicted people whose identity and self-esteem are centered in the continual accumulation of immediate, merchandised gratification.

Monstrous advertising campaigns begin conditioning new generations of hyper-consumers from infancy, molding them into needy, nagging children who grow up to be needy, nagging children.

Advertisers promote their stuff like its the ultimate solution that fires up prolonged pleasure. They try to get us to buy into a delusion that says to feel *this* we've got to have *that*.

For this ploy to work again and again, we need to be low consciousness. We need to have forgotten that what we feel emanates from what we're choosing to *be*.

All pleasure and pain expands from *within* us.

Now that only 18% of American television campaigns show a return on investment, perhaps educated people are onto the Madison Avenue mad mens' game.

It's an increasingly toxic and depleting game. We've got diminishing oil supplies, yet we still squander it to create mountains of packaging and throw-away plastic.

As a culture of harvest addicts, we barely notice industry harvesting the flesh and lungs off our planet's thin mantle—mostly to create mountains of trash going to landfills a few weeks after purchase.

The internet film *The Story of Stuff* (storyofstuff.com) estimates we're using less than three percent of what we buy six weeks after purchase. That means more than 97% of the natural resources we're stripping off the planet is engineered to be useless trash.

We can't keep this up!

Yet economists remain addicted to beliefs that happiness requires growing economies. If buying and addictive neediness isn't growing, economists say we're in trouble.

The growth of the globalization economy really only makes the richest 1% think they're happy.

For an economy to constantly grow, we the 99% have got to be indebted, needy, addictive, thoughtless and foreign to logic, reason, cause and effect, responsibility and higher Consciousness.

The collapse of corporations, banks, economies, and consumer confidence began with the collapse of higher Consciousness and the wisdom of Oneness.

The seed of crisis is the act of choosing to be unconscious of the results of our own beliefs and actions. It's choosing to be heartless and to not mind what our own business is destroying, while it creates.

None of us truly has peaceful well-being unless we all have peaceful well-being. It's the greedy close-minded *us*-and-*them* mentality that crumbles the foundations of nations.

Now we're crumbling the foundations of the planet. For sustainable quality of Life we've got to prioritize the eco of economy.

The Robbery of Oneness

The theft of Consciousness begins when any teacher, school, parental influence, or government fills any child's mind with the egotistic superiority of nationality, race, or species.

This rips the Oneness, the presence of life-loving innocence, out of our beings and firmly brands politicized paradigms of *us*-and-*them*, of nationalistic control agendas, and of the human ego's dark domination over everything.

Whenever any individual or organization tries to stratify worthiness, darkness shadows light, and the heart and mind are at risk of closing inward.

It is time to replace the ideologies of patriotism with a Consciousness of planetism. As the climate crisis, economic collapses and energy crisis shake us to our core, there will blossom an undeniable awareness that as the Presence of Creation's Consciousness, we're ALL on this precious planet equally together.

Any politicizing, ostracizing force that separates and alienates one class or race or nation from another, with any form of prejudice, bigotry, or conflict, is the darkness of ego activated as the chaos of destruction.

Biologists are witnessing the death of birth. Canadian broadcaster and zoologist Dr. David Suzuki says that 50,000 species throughout the food chain are going extinct every year. That's 137 species a day!

My beautiful place of ultra-Oneness with Creation's Consciousness has been my home, my floating sanctuary. This three bedroom home with its 18 foot ceilings floats on a mountain lake among Canada's majestic Pacific Coastal Mountains.

It is my pure, off-the-grid beautiful sanctuary, my floating Eden and the four summers I've spent writing this book there have been pure bliss.

In 2009, in this remote and pure region of clean Canada, we witnessed a shocking 90% drop in the salmon run on the Fraser River. I saw an equal drop in the number of fish seen on our lake. Neighbors speak of bees that have stopped producing honey. This has not happened before. For the first time, we don't awaken to morning calls of the loons. The loons are, as never before, silenced.

The ravages of industrial unconsciousness are mounting an assault on Life absolutely everywhere.

Meanwhile most people still think our problem is mismanagement of money. For Life to survive, economies must rejuvenate with higher Consciousness because this is a crisis of unconsciousness.

As I write this, there are 7 billion of us witnessing this Earth change. If we do not open our minds and hearts to live as One Life Loving harmonious Presence, millions of people will languish and die in purposeless chaos—not because of some wrathful judgement of Creation, but because of the low vibration of our mass Consciousness.

Life is this simple: everything is energy either becoming Life's expanding Light or collapsing into the darkness of unconscious chaos.

Symptoms of a Closed Mind

The only information that can squeeze into a closed mind must mesh with how that mind is already made up.

In a closed mind, information is judged by whether it shores up the fragile beliefs that already fester there. Closed-minded people need to *be* with like-minded people to feel comfortable in their own skin.

The painful pressure of always needing to feel right causes the mind to snap shut at the first hint of learning an inconvenient truth.

New information—and even questions—feel like attacks. To a closed mind, a new perspective, a new awareness of what's happening now, is threatening.

Closed minds age rapidly. They become nervous, stressed, guarded, and threatened by the evolution of Consciousness, energy and knowledge.

Any living energy presence cut off from its source dies. A stagnant pond, with no open flow of freshness, will eventually only support the simplest organisms before evaporating into such nothingness we'd hardly know it had ever been there at all.

Such are the lives of close-minded people.

The closed-mind cultures a swamp of fearful ego.

Ego collapses Life, it frays the very fabric of Creation. This is why we refer to a battle or fight as "entering the fray."

People with closed minds become mental amoebas. Single-mindedness makes them so learning-resistant that, even as they perish, they often intensify doing more of the same. They act much like a cancer that ultimately destroys itself by destroying its host.

There is nothing more destructive than an idea, if it's the only one you've got!

Adaptation is essential for long-term survival.

Closed minds stagnate—personally and collectively—in steps like these:

+ The mind closes in on an achievement strategy and works on it.
+ We get a fast start by plugging into people who match our popularized belief system. We're in the game! Hooray for us!
+ We apply the rules we were taught, and we score some points. It works! We are believers.
+ We partner and couple with those who are like-minded.
+ Life is good, and the mind closes shut. Firmly. We know how life works and how to work it. Time passes.
+ We're increasingly disturbed that people seem to be succeeding outside our box and without our old rules. Someone actually accuses us of "old school" tactics. They suggest we open up to what's happening now.
+ We keep on keeping on, always doing what we've always done. We're getting back less and less of what we've always gotten. So we do more of the same, only harder.
+ Doing more of the same harder yields diminishing returns.
+ The energy in and around our relationships is dying.

- Change becomes the enemy. The world seems trendy and fickle and crazy. We wonder what's happening. We're mad because "they've" all gone mad.
- Younger, creative types with their shallow, trendy tricks are winning at the game now, with less substance and with less of what seems real!
- We feel nobody knows what's good anymore. It's all going off in crazy directions.
- It becomes an us-verses-them game of choosing sides and sticking to our guns. It's a politicized war now, and to win we're going in for the kill, keeping our nose to the grindstone and our eye on the prize. However, the prize needs to be lower than the grindstone for us to keep an eye on it.
- The quality of everything, from relationships to health to career, is stressed-out and in rapid decay. Militarization grows while endings, demises, and deaths happen all around us on what has become this battlefield of Life.
- Our Old School is losing the war.
- Opening our eyes every morning feels sad and scary. Our dwindling number of insiders speak the language of embattled losers.
- We're using substances to barely get through these miserable days. It feels like we're in a Death Valley of evil, without fresh water. (Although alcohol seems to be doing the trick for now.)
- We wonder how life got so sour, and then we surrender to beliefs that it's all going to Hell. And so our Life does go to Hell, little by little, piece by piece, one wretched moment at a time.

+ The saga of a closed-mind lurches through these stages, often in random order, and perhaps through many jobs, careers, addictions, relationships and marriages. Close-minded people eventually feel very small and their lives get smaller too.

The Elasticity of Old Habits

One of the greatest challenges of overcoming an addiction is the elastic pull of familiarity.

Familiarity pulls us back into habitual behaviors where we think we're "safely" incubated from the flow of pressures to learn, change, grow and *be* more of Life. When something changes everything in our lives, and the closed-mind refuses to open to the dawning of a new reality, we usually retreat into a darkened room and remain there until we can face the light of day. Life grows in The Light.

The Old School, that believes the bottom line is money, often retreats to rooms devoid of sunlight and flowing, fresh air. Their boardrooms, clubs, bars and restaurants are often dark caverns cut off from the energies that create Life.

I frequently appreciate how values and decisions change when we meet outside on a hill with a glorious view of Nature, or among people in the places where our decisions will have the most impact.

The Old School makes important decisions deep within the secretive high security chambers of these wizards of our Oz.

How many capital cities of nations are located in the mountainous majesty of Nature?

Almost all national capitols are in carefully chosen flat places where the monuments humans build to themselves are the biggest creations on the horizon. Nature dwarfs the creations of humans.

With an open, conscious mind we're flowing and connecting with artistry, creativity, beauty and possibilities of nature in harmony with humanity. Combine these powers of now, with the wisdom of sustainable success from the past, and you're being Our Renaissance of Consciousness.

Theme Parks of An Open Mind

An open mind that Loves Life Loves what Creation's Consciousness creates. Love the Creation that IS LIFE!

ALL of it!

Open your gratitude and Love for ALL THAT IS now, including what you've judged to be chaos! Just surrender and open.

Now you are being and creating peace. Being open-minded gratitude uplifts you to Oneness with Creation.

The energies that collapse Creation aren't money or influence. The black hole of Creation is addictions—the competitive, comparative greed and ego of low consciousness. This is true among artists, leaders and ALL of Creation.

Let's be students of blissful happiness. Think for a moment about the happiest and most conscious, joyful people you know.

Are they the richest and thinnest people you know?

No, they're the life-loving grateful people who see each day as an adventure in Creation's endlessly creatively entertaining theme park.

Opening their eyes in the morning is their ticket to ride. Wherever they are has the potential to be their happiest place on Earth. They're non-comparative and non-competitive, open-minded and generous-of-spirit. All kinds of people and energies are attracted to them.

These joyful people are Loved because they Love Life. These cherished artists of *being* are your greatest teachers.

What's your theme park these days?

Spend a little time with that answer. Go deep.

You are creating yourself and your future with the energies of your thoughts and beliefs.

The theme park of my mind is Creation's Consciousness; it's a beautiful place to *be* day after day. It ALL keeps opening up and getting better.

Blossoming Consciousness is like that.

COME ONE, COME ALL!

STEP RIGHT UP TO
CREATION'S THEME PARK
OF CONSCIOUSNESS!

ENJOY FOR AS LONG
AS YOU LIKE,
AN ETERNITY
IF YOU CHOOSE.

WE ONLY GO DARK
ON THE DAYS
YOUR MIND CLOSES!

An open-minded child
taught to *be* higher
Consciousness,
and to respect and Love
ALL Life,
will not stand for, march for,
or murder for
the tyranny of big business.

The Light Illuminates An Open Mind

Small minds are easily influenced, distracted and controlled. They obsess over personality rather than quality of being. They're filled and entertained by superficial appearances and gossip rather than quality of content.

Closed minds become self-absorbed and filled with ego. They fear, worry and obsess about what doesn't matter, constantly trying to fill themselves from the outside in.

At the turn of this century, when a comparative, competitive self-absorbing preoccupation was the Westernized norm, a greedy aristocracy occupied and ruled the land without its people being the higher Consciousness of logic and reason.

I write this to echo awareness far forward through time, to you, for Life's future.

When peace and prosperity have pacified us, mothers and fathers, and their sons and daughters forget what the stench of fear and the control-hungry egos of tyrants smell, sound, feel and look like.

For tyrants to grip the land in a stranglehold of fear, the indifferent silence of grandmothers and grandfathers is required.

It is the responsibility of the elders to be worthy of respect and to awaken the conscious awareness, the kindness of the young—and to celebrate individuality and creativity and open the Presence of high Consciousness, the Love of Loving Life—in even the most different, lost and fearful among us.

A child who Loves Loving ALL Life will not stand for, march for, or murder for any tyrants.

It is in the hearts and minds of our children that peaceful prosperity, Consciousness, is born through nurturing.

It is the unloved and angry young that are the most influenced and recruitable for the dark campaigns of the influential. Tyranny's march to power is to first identify enemies, spread fear, militarize and infect the dumbed-down media and schools.

Tyrants get to us to get the best of us.

Their seductive propaganda convinces peaceful families that peace requires war. They argue that prolonged peaceful prosperity demands domination and conflicts.

We all parent the mass consciousness.

With logic and reason, trust and communication unplugged from higher Consciousness, the evil of fear infects the mass Consciousness as we're dumbed down and seduced with sugar-coated, smartly uniformed, deadly weapons of mass destruction.

Nonsense!

Nonsense is what doesn't make sense.

Nonsense is the unconscious self-destructiveness and doom of industrialized militarism and wealth-addicted wars against humanity and Life on this planet. That's the nonsense!

But how did we get Life so upside down?

Tyrants convince us we must satisfy their agendas to have happiness and peace. They dumb down our Consciousness with stressful, anxious hyper-consuming. They extinguish the enlightenment of global Oneness by narrowing our Cosmic Presence and straight-jacketing us into believing tribal egocentric pride creates quality of Life.

That's the apple in our Garden of Eden!

We've declared war on Life with militaries and economies addicted to growth.

This nonsense violates Creation's energies and that's why civilizations implode into their own greed. They implode not because Creation has a judgmental or vengeful personality. They implode because unconscious, violent, greedy abuse collapses the Life flow of any system.

Violent, destructive, unconscious history can only repeat itself if grandmothers and grandfathers, mothers and fathers, forfeit higher Consciousness for lifestyle.

Competing and comparing, jealousy and fear bring out the worst in us, and military and spiritual tyrants need us to *be* at our worst.

Tyrants militarize humanity's capacity for low consciousness—and through *being* that, doom happens.

Love Loving Life!

Life, peace, and diplomacy always begin with humility, kindness, listening and learning from others. Being this co-creates compassionate win-win-win breakthrough solutions. Breaking through the pain of fearing and destroying is cause for celebrating humanity's victory over the chaos of fearing ourselves. That celebrating is not nonsense, it is the rejuvenating blossoming of LIFE!

Enlighten Darkness

If fear-infected social paralysis tries to get you, *be* the courage of higher Consciousness. Open your Consciousness of Creation's Oneness and Love Life, no matter what you're faced with. You'll cleanse the moment and lift yourself into the energy realms of higher dimensions.

Being that blossoming of higher Consciousness is our eternal purpose and possibility!

Open up your blossoming enlightenment and feel what opens unto you, through you.

As pure, expansive Presence, you're a powerfully radiant Consciousness, a Cosmic orgasm!

In the face of fear and darkness *be* enlightened higher Consciousness and allow it to flow as your thoughts, feelings, words and actions. Let compassion be your guide.

Darkness cannot penetrate Light. Light penetrates darkness, and when it does, energy is activated, and Life happens.

It's all energy, and THE LIGHT Loves Life!

It's that simple!

BE THE LIGHT!

Children grow up to be tyrants of destructive darkness because they don't trust Love and higher Consciousness. They become the fear and doubt that make minds and hearts go dark. They've not learned to trust simply *being* expansive gratitude and Love.

Let us help one another learn that trust.

In the face of fear, *be* enlightening, expanding higher Consciousness and experience how you and others are lifted up.

It ALL really is that simply beautiful.

CHAPTER 6

Transcendence

Being alive as the Presence of authentic energies rather than through labels, words, or materialism is to *be* transcendence.

transcendence | trøn(t)'sɛndəns | noun

> Above or beyond the range of merely physical or normal human experience: *the search for a transcendent level of knowledge* surpassing the ordinary; and opening to the exceptional.

Rather than identifying everything through hollow words or concepts, transcendence connects you *as* energy *to* energy. It is the clearest and most connectively creative way of *being*.

Life relates to Life as energy, not words.

Everything is energy, it's all ENERGY! When you connect your Presence of Consciousness, with the energy you're focusing on, remarkable possibilities happen.

Two Minute Healing

BE It

Complete the following sentence in your mind, "I really Love _____."

What did you feel? Did the words or thoughts uplift you?

Now experience transcendence.

Love isn't the word, it is *being* the energy.

Think of what you deeply love again.

Now really feel the Love, open it up; open up the Love. Open it through your heart, through your mind, and completely through your whole Presence and really *be* Love.

Let the Love expand, and let its energy fill you and radiate out from you.

Take deep breaths and let the Love open up.

Do this now and experience how transcendent you are when you're *BE*ing Love.

Saying the name is hollow compared to *being* its energy. Our words are nothing compared to the energies.

To live as transcendence is to mingle your authentic Consciousness energies, the Presence of your eternal self with the energies of everything you think of, believe, value or encounter. It connects you with Life as Life. This is how you were as a young child until you were unplugged from energies and you lost your senses.

As children we experience the whole world as energy, but we're soon taught it's inappropriate to let big energies and feelings swell up in us. We're then taught to relate to the world more and more through cold, institutional words, and we feel less and less—until we don't feel much anymore at all.

As our child awareness of purely *being* was taken away it was replaced with working and getting.

When you are transcendent and relating to Life through energy rather than just words, you've returned to your senses, instincts, awareness, and an experiential knowing that is pure and empowered by the energies of what's-happening-now. This is how animal instincts function.

As we venture through uncharted territories, these are the skills for survival.

Energizing a Community

In the new economy of conscious commerce, transcendence is vital for sustaining a community. Most people in business and government get consumed by busy-ness or numbers rather than awakening to the energies of how things really are—NOW!

Business was militarized, employees were taught to keep noses to the grindstone and to shut common senses down. Managers lost good sense and functioned at low and destructive levels of unconsciousness.

I offer the insights of my transcendence: my abilities to research and feel the energies and experience something for what it is now. I use trend-tracking skills that let me know where circumstances were vis-à-vis where they are. Through that energy tracking I can tell communities where potentials are going and suggest ways to manage them. These seemingly prophetic abilities involve transcendence, an intimate relationship with energies that we can all access.

Consumer confidence is a shifting, moody energy that business publishes as numbers. It's the vapors of where masses of people were. However, people attuned to local energies are infinitely more aware, connected, and capable of feeling changes and values shifts.

Transcendence lifts you above the anchors of mere words and numbers into the realms of pure energy, and that's where Truth is.

Many dogs and cats immediately recognize and avoid dark-hearted people because animals read energies. Animals don't have the blinders that pedigree reading people do.

Dogs and cats have a clear read on character because vibrational energy and scent reveal the truth of someone.

Do you suppose aristocracies started powdering and perfuming so nobody could smell a rat?

Beyond Polarity

Higher Consciousness is not polarized. It is other than, immune from the polarization by which all atoms, all matter, and weakened minds are aligned.

If you've listened to the Transcendence audio program in The Mind Spa at consciousworldsummit.com, you've already experienced the liberation of transcendence.

It lifts you to the realms of energy, so that rather than *being* distracted by the mind's random thoughts, you're *being* the flow of authentic energies.

As transcendence, the limiting veils of words, worth, and time drop away. We open to the realms of orchestrating energies where everything is. We're meant to *be* there to receive, regularly.

Transcendent Consciousness gives you deep, rich, and knowing experiences. Instinct, intuition, psychic knowing, and the Consciousness of what you're connecting to enriches your being. You're functioning at levels far above—and more connective than—the laws of attraction.

Liberate yourself from the anchors of mere words. From that lofty realm, feel the energy of what other people are communicating, and you will develop the awareness of someone who has an excellent "take" on people, agendas, organizations, possibilities and the future.

When an experience is really beautiful and touching, open your mind and heart to fully be the energy of that moment. Let it really open up through you as you.

This is profoundly healing and energizing.

Experiment with your ability to experience things purely energetically, and as you gradually learn to trust that ability, let the authentic energies guide your values and choices. The rejuvenation of quality of Life, the creation of sustainable communities, Our Renaissance of Consciousness will happen through people attuned to the qualities of energies.

Transcendence opens your authenticity. You'll discover that people feel safer with you and closer to you. Where there used to be conflict, there is renewed togetherness. Issues and differences vaporize in the light of anyone who has transcendently given up pettiness.

By opening your heart to Love Loving Life, and ALL the amazing energy moments, sensations, lessons and experiences of being, you heal your relationship with yourself and with Creation.

We cannot give what we do not have. If you don't have an expansively grateful and Loving relationship with your own *being*, and with Totality, how can you have a deeply good relationship with anyone or anything?

Transcendence lifts us up to Love the expansive depth of goodness.

As low, unconsciousness we're battling with, and feeling attacked by practically everything.

Being transcendent you're actively expanding and co-creating what you Love, and in the light of that, what used to be big issues shrink to being just the small stuff. Transcendence liberates you, lifting you for a time, above the stuff that pulls your spirit down.

You're freed of everything gravitational, to later return to the day's doings with higher Consciousness, awareness, resiliency and flow.

When you choose to Love Loving Life, the energies of Life and the way Creation simply, beautifully and elegantly creates opens to you, through you.

This is what all great teachers of spirituality encouraged us to *be*.

When your *being* is transcendently freed from ego you're partnering with Creation as Creation.

Try *being* transcendence with the energy of a sunrise or sunset. Rather than just looking at beauty open to *being* it, to absorbing it, to mingling your *being* with its *being*.

Last night, after writing this chapter, I dreamt the following story.

The Presence

A man was sitting with a young boy at the end of a dock. They were looking across a beautiful lake at the radiant sunset, Creation's light show, celebrating the release of the day.

"Do you see the beauty and the creativity and the colors of this moment?", the man asked the quiet boy.

The boy gazed all around at everything bathed in a rose hue. To him it looked like a goodnight kiss from the sky.

"Yes, I see!", said the boy.

The man said, "Now feel it, feel the colors of the sky and everything around you as if it is ALL you, because it is. The same Life artistry that is making this moment for me and you to share is also making us as this moment. We're the art too, we're ALL one Creation."

"I feel that!", said the boy. "I feel it!"

"That glorious beauty out there is inside you, too. Your Presence can have as much bigness and color and energy and space and possibility as the sky! There is no separation. It's all pure unlimited Creation. And no matter what name someone gives it, we all feel and Love BEing THE PRESENCE!"

"Wow! I'm that big?", wondered the boy.

"You're bigger. You're much bigger if you choose to fully BE! People will try to make you feel separate and small, but your Consciousness is as bright and big as you let it be. Your Light is as bright as that sky and even bigger."

"Yes", said the boy. "I am."

CHAPTER 7
Presence

What we've considered a wise and knowing presence of mind is actually Presence of Consciousness.

People of higher Consciousness have an enchanting composure. They bring something great, something exceptional, to the moment.

They're not small or petty. They're bigger than small-minded, immature, high school power plays, and so they don't get caught up in them.

Higher Consciousness makes us etherial and earthy and that can be sensual and alluringly sexy.

People *being* Presence ask insightful questions that create deeper connective understandings. They offer reasoned choices that draw from the big picture and the greater good of all.

BEing the Presence of higher Consciousness allows us to be generous of spirit, flowing with compassion, enthusiasm, wisdom, gratitude, and the enlightenment that emanates externally what we're composed of internally.

Living as Presence, your awareness mingles with the Consciousness orchestrating everything—you're receiving from the Big Picture and flow of Life.

You naturally did this as a child. You connected as energy with the energy of everything around you. Life was a big, stimulating energy experiment, until you were taught to use words, and you began experiencing Life through knowing brands and values rather than the energy.

Our Eternal Now

Now is all we have, all we'll ever have. Now is all there authentically is.

So, *be* here now. Let go of the past and the future, let go of all judgements and stress and *be* peace with Now, just as everything is.

Allow your *being* to be peace in this moment as this moment and feel how that feels.

We are Presence regardless of whether our Consciousness is in a body or freed by death to fully *BE* spirit.

> "Life has no opposite.
> The opposite of death is birth."
>
> Eckhart Tolle

Death is not the opposite of *being*. There is no opposite of Presence.

Death is the conclusion of birth.

The expansion of Creation's Consciousness through each of us is the heart of the matter, the point of being!

Through my second "near death" experience, I received the following awareness: as enlightening Consciousness, we're attuned to more expansive, and flowingly creative energy stratas. This is our possibility and purpose.

Science and medicine are realizing that all living things emit a radioactivity and highly refined light— what I'm describing as active Consciousness.

It's an etherial light beyond normal light.

Sunlight penetrates, activates and organizes darkness into Life.

A bright white light's beam energizes and nourishes plants with its high vibrational clarity.

Bright light radiates more energy than a dull, weak light.

If your Life's inner light is dimmed by unresolved shame for your past or unfounded fears for your future, your essence is stretched, warped, torn and not focused with Now. When you're being worry about numbers, appearances, status or stuff, you're shrunken, imprisoned and not free to *be* expansive, enlightened Presence flowing with the beauty and creative possibilities of Now!

You've robbed yourself of Now!

If we're not opening our Presence, the huge possibilities of today pass us by. When we're sweating the small stuff, solutions pass us by.

Yes, we need to manage our finances and accumulated responsibilities. However, when we are owned and trapped by the *trappings of success*, we're imprisoned—just managing to get by. When that happens, we're small, dim, afraid, addictive, needy and unconscious—we don't flow, we don't shine, we don't attract from vibrations of higher Consciousness, and problems grow faster than solutions.

When we're not openly, energetically and co-creatively being presence, the potentials of coincidence and synchronicity are restricted from flowing through us. We end up feeling cheated, angry, brittle and starved.

Without an open mind and expansive Presence we age rapidly and everything can feel like a pointless exercise. We start believing and *being* doom and gloom.

Think of someone you know who has a dark cloud over them—someone who is petty and needy, criticizing, comparative, complaining and depressed.

They probably believe that what they need is lots of money, but no amount of money will rid them of their misery, because that's the vibrational energy of their *being*. Their beliefs, values and choices create their misery.

I've known miserable billionaires whose wealth, status and possessions became their prison—and they're simply too rich, trapped and addicted to get themselves out.

Presence opens flow with what Creation has in mind.

Quality of *being* creates quality of experience.

Presence is your authentic vibration, your radiant contribution of Consciousness, your true *musical note* adding to the symphony of the Universe—our one song of *BE*ingness.

Opportunity, possibilities, solutions and sustainable sensuality are attracted to the Presence of higher consciousness because it's connective, intuitive, compassionate, creatively playful, wise, and deeply sensual. It's alluring, fascinating, earthy, authentic Presence that creates lasting attraction and sustainability.

It's the chemistry of trusting, lasting, Loving relationships. To know such a relationship, *be* the kindness, higher Consciousness and authentic Love of Presence.

As expansive Consciousness, we arrive for Life! Our relationships become a sustainable symphony of *being*.

This is why quality of Consciousness creates quality of experience.

Humans Co-create or Destroy

Holding your Presence opens you to being whole and unified with Creation's Oneness—your awareness is opened to sensing the pushes and pulls of energies and choices and you're wisely able to feel and gauge how a destructive choice will play out.

Courtrooms and prisons are packed with people who've lost their Presence and acted out the chaos of unconsciousness.

When we drop down out of Presence, we can make regrettable choices that change our quality of Life. We live for the moment, lose our senses and go out of our minds, only to follow and please someone we know isn't very conscious.

Without Presence, we can't trust ourselves because we lose control of ourselves.

Without Presence, we can be easily fooled.

Without Presence, humans doom themselves.

The Children of Industry

As young children we're witty, bright lights who naturally, enthusiastically Love being. But societies, addicted to industrial globalizing growth, rob children of higher Consciousness, forcing them to abandon their unique one-of-a-kind passionate, creative light-of-Life.

The industrial age taught us to fit in, to think and act like assembly line machinery, cogs in the wheels of the industrial agenda to pave the planet with strip mall, franchised commerce.

For many dark-age centuries, greedy male dominated aristocracies successfully suppressed the heartfelt wisdom of grounded women, the sensibilities, flavors, scents and artistry of differing races and cultures, and the creative artistry of homosexuals.

Greedy male dominated aristocracies forced us to need them, to judge, shun, compete, compare and to nervously keep buying what enriched them.

At the core of this is a complete lack of faith in the Consciousness within each person. Rather than allowing humanity to openly and simply *be* peaceful, openhearted and grateful Life Loving families, their political campaigns made our lives living Hells.

Being possessed by judging, competing, comparing and possessing turns us into small, petty, needy and addictive people. And that's how tyrants need us to be.

Our generations' Renaissance of Consciousness is the letting go of that bad dream—it's the end of *being* the pawns of greed.

It's Life's hope for itself.

Expanded and enlightened, your Consciousness is infinitely greater than you've been taught to believe. The essence of you, that light, is not a piece of your mother's Presence, or a piece of your father's. You are a complete, unique Light of glowing creative Consciousness delivered through your parents.

The mother and father through whom you were born did not create your essence. You came through them but you are not *of* them.

You are a spark of Consciousness,
Creation's dream,
the pure Presence of
Life's possibility
in every given moment
as every given moment.

You are The Light of Life, the ongoing Big Bang.
Life's Source is *BE*ing you as you are *BE*ing it!
You are Creation, and there is no separation.

What beautiful and Life loving adventure are
you not giving yourself permission to feel and *be*?

What do you serve by imprisoning this
possibility?

You exist in this vastly beautiful and Lovable
Life plan. With each fresh breath, your Presence
is a one-of-a-kind original creation.

To take a first step to opening Presence, take a
long, slow deep breath using all of your lung
capacity. And as you exhale, let go of judgments
and *be* peace with Now. Relax all resistance in
your mind and body. The job of *being* God is
already taken, so let go of the battles and open
your Presence to *be* peace with ALL, just as
everything is now.

Let the energy of your heart's *being*, that inner
Light that is you, open and expand.

And allow your Presence to be One with
your world.

You are Life's Light, Life's hope and possibility for Life, constantly refreshing itself through your Presence with NOW.

BE Life!

BE Life's ongoing, original, creatively entertaining rejuvenation.

BE the magnificence of higher Consciousness and feel Life's beauty open up through you and to you.

How We Lost Presence

Before the toxically successful Industrial Revolution, communities of earthy people maintained a respectful, symbiotic relationship with the delicate balances of Nature, the land, weather and the seasons. Interdependent Oneness with Nature is central to quality of Life. We still need Presence, instincts, wisdom, creativity, resourcefulness and community to survive.

The Industrial Age clouded our mass Consciousness with bigness and smoke, fire and fear. Wizards of industry and investment ruled our Oz and everything turned the color of money.

Our focus shifted from gratitude for the bountiful beauty and grace of each day, to getting those assembly line, advertised, branded and packaged products. We began living in a dollar-driven, money-makes-the-world-go-around, parallel reality.

Idolizing globalized industrialization turns humans into lost, uncreative, addictive, greedy harvest addicts. Before industrialization, more than enough was too much. After industrialization, enough wasn't enough.

Alienated from the delicate wisdom of Creation's Consciousness, and the beautiful simplicities of living gently with Nature, concepts of happiness and self worth got attached to getting those shiny new assembly line products. Our mass addictions to bigger and newness dragged us hook, product line and sinker into the depths of debt's disheartenment.

What promised to be the globalization of the great American dream collapsed into nightmares of greed.

Greed collapses goodness.

The American dream wasn't about happiness or well-being. It wasn't a quality-centered dream at all. It wasn't about *being* anything good or worthwhile—it was all about getting.

The American dream, fashioned for us by the mad men of Madison Avenue and the wily of Wall Street, is need and greed fueled. It banks on us wanting things we haven't even seen yet, and applying layers of artificial happiness from the outside in.

Does that ever work?

No.

Advertising frenzied hyper-consuming, and living in a house of credit cards, has dumbed down creativity, talent, reason and logic.

Mass consciousness was so dumbed down that people bartered their Presence to the profiteers.

We learned to buy our feelings, rather than to simply *be* the feelings we desire. We became human doings, human havings, rather than human BEings.

Our sense of decency became a casualty of conspicuously competitive consumption.

Imitating the lifestyles of the rich and famous caught on. *"Better"* was defined as *"more."*

Executive piracy began leveraging mortgage debt into slavery.

The 1960s possibility of peace and Loving Oneness was a teaser for The Occupation Movements and Our Community of Consciousness.

The 1960s energized the civil rights movement, equality for women, anti-war Consciousness and activism, as well as many counter-cultures.

It was a time for liberating Love, social experimentation and spiritual exploration.

Masses of letter-writing, vocal people took to the streets to protest the unconsciousness of the Vietnam War, and it ended. Young people regarded that War and "The Establishment" as clear evidence that the older generations were on a misguided path of greed and doom.

But the 1960s social era of hope and optimism was clobbered again and again, mortified by three assassinations, two Kennedys and a King. America's teachers of Consciousness and hope were assassinated. It was a police state nightmare in full view. We were stunned into a stupefied silence, and masses of us used alcohol and drugs to cope with the darkness.

Deadly new addictive drugs that stupefied users suddenly became widely available. And while the chemistry of plastics changed products, dastardly designer drugs clenched our emotions and Consciousness. Hippies experimented with better-living-through-chemistry and then lost themselves.

Consciousnesses-numbing anti-depressants stun and zombify many of us to this day.

Evil could murder courageous leaders of Consciousness in full view, and masses of post-traumatic-stress tranquilized consumers, addicted to lifestyle, would cower in an awkwardly compromised comfort.

The children of flower power, and their children, became hyper-consumers for all they were worth —and more.

Big government, owned by bigger business, became Big Brother. The U.S. Federal Government discovered that, from time to time, shock-and-awe terrorizes and paralyses people so that, during the confusion, influence and wealth can be stratified up to those who wag the dog with bigness, fire, smoke and fear.

While this agenda played out repeatedly, drug industries released newer generations of benzodiazepines, tranquilizers and muscle-relaxants that numb Consciousness and corkscrew our emotions ever more deeply. The slew of drugs that followed gave birth to a nation of addicts and legal drug cartels.

People changed, children were educated to be passive, emotionally adolescent extensions of machines rather than thinking, reasoning, logical adults.

The military-industrial complex created enough weaponry to kill every person on the planet ten times, and the masses largely remained unconsciously, obediently mute.

Profiteering wars are the big business of the mass destruction industry. The military contractors, those pirates of peace, are halted when enough people rise up and go out into the streets to call it what it is—evil, flag sanctioned massacre.

Then, peace returns.

In the aftermath of The Vietnam War, we were carefully taught to play with our deck of credit cards and to buy the gadgets and pharmaceuticals in all those pretty commercials.

We bought shiny new cars and bigger and
bigger dolled-up houses to polish up with all those
new and improved soaps; and on Kodachrome, for
a while, we looked like happy Barbies and Kens—
not too fat yet.

But there was a growing emptiness behind our
eyes. We'd lost our Presence, our connection to
Source.

We'd sold out the very Presence that
harmonizes the human condition—the decency
that makes us comfortable in our own skin and
within the Oneness of ALL.

The Industrial Age's globalization disconnected
mass Consciousness from the planet—from the
symbiotic Oneness of Nature and our fragile
biosphere. We became alien to how Life creates,
and alien to ourselves, the Presence of
Consciousness that is us.

We lived as needy, greedy, comparative,
competitive addictive shells ready to do each
other in for ego and instant gratification.

Corporate lenders with sights set no higher than
quarterly profits were willing to greedily do in
their neighbors and to sink the economies of
fellow nations with ticking-time-bomb mortgages
set to implode families and then the whole global
economy.

One percent of the population had rigged the
global economy to funnel vast amounts of wealth
and influence up to them.

And the dumbed down masses didn't see how
our walk-in closets filled with those big brands,
bought in the big chain stores, shackle us with
debt and despair as they kill local creativity and
community.

No one quite knows what year community died.

The highest price is paid when greed
undermines quality of being. Loss of higher

Consciousness is the beginning of the end of any civilization.

As mass Consciousness was dumbed down further and further, we became the cancer cells of our own planet—unconscious to the reality that we're killing our host.

Of course we're very different and more intelligent than cancer cells. They can't build radiation devices that can wipe them out.

We can and we do.

I publish these words now, so future generations may understand that human history has never repeated itself—it's unconscious people who repeat history.

Without the Presence of higher Consciousness, the delicate balance of humanity and Nature, the dance we do for a brilliant flash of a Lifetime, amounts to nothing but ruins.

Things have to get bad enough for masses of people to stop following the antics of the *wanna be* leaders and *BE* the change.

"Reality does have a way of knocking at the door."

Al Gore
Nobel laureate, author

As I write this, 50,000 species throughout the food chain are going extinct every year. This dark age of human unconsciousness may be followed by the dawning of humanity's greatest possibility, if we each lift the mass Consciousness by *being* the change and Presence of higher Consciousness.

If masses of people support local conscious commerce, we'll rejuvenate quality of Life community by community.

The Great Transformation to a high consciousness, low-carbon economy will be a driver of conscious commerce and economic prosperity. Embarking on this journey to heal humanity's relationship with our world and save Life's future can, according to leading experts, create tens of millions of new jobs—including whole new professions.

The choices of our generations are awesome. Our mass consciousness now has endless ramifications for the future of quality of Life.

> "It is in the hands of the present generation: a decision we cannot escape, and a choice to be mourned or celebrated through all the generations that follow."
>
> Al Gore
> from *Our Choice: A Plan To Save The Climate Crisis*
> (Rodale, 2009)

We must develop affordable, efficient, clean energies and bring into our future only the best practices of the agricultural, industrial and information ages to co-create Life's sustainability.

Our greatest inventors and creative minds need to be pulled off the creation of weaponry and repurposed to co-create Life's sustainability.

The coal and oil industries spend big to muddy science and confuse people. Greed and growth-addicted business twist truth into politicizing wedges that confuse discussions, stall solutions and leverage chaos...this agenda attacks the very heart of Life's possibility for itself.

It is high time for humanity to clean up its actions and this social movement needs you.

> "Unless someone like you
> cares a whole awful lot,
> nothing is going to get better.
> It's not."
>
> The Onceler
> from Dr. Suess's
> eco-children's
> classic *The Lorax*

The turning point that has become Life's tipping point began with the pollution of our Presence of *being*.

The change must happen within us.

Higher Consciousness doesn't promise some newfangled Americanized dream—it leads us to simply, peacefully and gratefully *BE* Life Loving Life.

We've got to come back to the garden.

Presence Delivers Well-Being

Flow, synchronicity, grace and Love are delivered through Presence. Arrive for your Life as Presence, and Life flows to and through you.

*BE*ing higher Consciousness doesn't happen in your mind. The mind is just electricity: it cannot create any more identity or Presence in you than it can in your computer.

> "Knowing yourself deeply
> has nothing to do with the
> ideas floating around in
> your mind. Knowing yourself
> is to be rooted in being,
> instead of lost in your mind."
>
> Eckhart Tolle
> spiritual teacher, author

Consciousness is the joyful, adventurous Life Source you lived as a creative, aware, passionate and playful young child—until it was deliberately and strategically disconnected.

Then, when you'd let go of yourself, of your conscious awareness, and learned to obediently follow the leader, you were classified among the "well-adjusted" children.

Obviously children need to be taught and socialized, but the old paradigm's education system was rigged in favor of the 1%, and they needed the 99% to be unaware of it.

The Unconscious Economy

Recent aristocracies have strategically boxed us in. We were supposed to find happiness cooped inside dark, solemn chambers designed by egocentric, competitive, comparative, politically power-hungry men.

Aristocracies taught us to be indebted and enslaved masses, obediently filing into classrooms and then cubicles to be bean-counting, dollar-chasing, cross-addicted, functionary number-crunchers.

As dumbed-down digit-thinkers, we lived that greed-driven parallel reality to the brink of disaster.

As young children of brilliant Consciousness, we were trained to follow-the-leader, to stop opening our minds and hearts to daydreams, and to put our noses to the grindstone. Inside the monumental boxes and soul-suffocating mouse cubicles of the big business, religion, government, military complex, with our noses to the grindstone, we can't see, appreciate or *BE* Life's big picture! We don't consciously witness what we're doing to ourselves.

During the darkness just before the dawn, the U.S. created a "No Child Left Behind" centered education system that chained teachers and students to tests that quantified dumbed-down digit-thinkers.

After some of my live presentations, teachers have approached me to speak of their despair and depression over not being able to inspire the whole child. They say logic, reasoning, the instincts of intuition and creativity got left behind by No Child Left Behind.

> "What's troubling is that our system is obsessed with standardization at the very time when the future of our economy depends on the opposite."
>
> Daniel Pink
> author of *A Whole New Mind: Why Right-Brainers Will Rule The Future*

Without open-minded higher Consciousness, our spirits and minds become so spatially small and closed that only small awareness and ideas can fit in.

Inside the boxed mind is exactly how centuries of greed-addicted aristocracies have needed their enslaved, indebted, nervous, judged and suffering masses to be.

Now we know that the agendas of industrial and information age education, government, and globalizing business are not quality-of-Life centered.

Following old-economy leaders, unplugged from Consciousness, we are doomed. Being the unconsciousness of a greed-addicted, Nature conquering, money-makes-the-world-go-around parallel reality, we are anti-Life.

Greed fueled constant industrialized growth is anti-life.

The stranglehold of those dark ages is releasing its grip.

We're discovering higher Consciousness is the key that opens Creation's possibilities. The invitation of our Community of Consciousness is to regain Consciousness and rejuvenate communities in new ways.

Presence Opens Oneness

ALL of Creation's creatures connect through Consciousness.

Yesterday I rode a new friend's horse along trails meandering through a mature rain forest. It was magnificent. I opened my mind and held my Presence of Consciousness during this gentle ride.

The horse's owner said she'd never seen "Boots" so relaxed. All I had to do was *feel* turning left or right with my Presence and he would feel and do it too. At each fork in the trail he would pause and ask, with his Presence, which way are we going. I only had to feel the direction we were to go and we'd go!

At one juncture his head turned to the far right, and an image of big apples popped into my awareness. Up that winding trail, Boots walked me right under the tree in the perfect spot for me to shake a branch so juicy apples dropped all around us and we shared the feast.

Horse whisperers center themselves as Presence.

In your home, the next time you have an insect or bird needing to go outside, expand your Consciousness and *be* your Presence.

Open doors or windows for its exit route, and send out a Conscious message that helps this creature go outside. Feel how good it will feel for it to *be* outside again.

If you need to carry it outside, hold your Presence of Consciousness and fill your awareness with your Loving intention to set it free...outside. Feel how it feels to *be* out in nature and calmly offer it a ride.

As Consciousness, you're a bug whisperer!

You'll be amazed at how all creatures relax when they're in the peaceful Presence of Consciousness.

The Presence of ALL

The brilliant quantum physicist David Bohm worked with Albert Einstein and wrote twenty-four books. He said, "Matter has mental properties as well as physical properties."

He taught us that every particle has a rudimentary mind-like quality.

Since everything is made of the *same* basic micro-elements dancing to the symphony of Creation Consciousness—the morphic field of Presence is what makes it what it was, and is, and is becoming.

Science is proving that when Presence interacts with the energies around us we influence the morphic field in limitless ways.

Late in life David Bohm became a close friend of the Dalai Lama, the profoundly healing teacher who says, "My religion is kindness."

We will fully *be* humanity's renaissance when each of us is the peaceful Consciousness that opens us to Oneness with Creation's Presence.

Try Loving Life as nonjudgemental, grateful Oneness with ALL Life, just the way Creation is creating it here, there and everywhere. You'll discover that you bring to Life harmony, prosperity and creativity.

Imagine a future when the media stops polluting with divisive judgments, competing and comparing; and you live as a Life Loving Presence that celebrates ALL of Life's ongoing creativity. Imagine that! Feel that!

You can *be* that now. You can heal your *being* by letting go of judgments, competing, comparing and hyper-controlling. Allow the armor around your heart, the anger around your heart, to melt away now. Open your heart to Loving Life in this moment as this moment.

Surrender the battle and Love Loving Life!

Feel how it opens up to you, through you, as you.

When we stop the struggling and simply Love Life's infinite creativity and live harmoniously with it, as it, we heal our relationship with Creation.

When we let go of the ego's addiction to controlling and simply allow, we drop the tight guardedness around our heart and appreciate every moment's infinitely entertaining Creativity.

When we consciously drop our guardedness, melt the armor around our hearts and open gratitude we become the change, we become peace—we unite with Creation's Consciousness. Then Presence opens up to us, through us.

When Something Changes Everything

When a dramatic, traumatic change impacts our fearful and controlling ego, we're shattered into pieces. We're out of our minds with grief because an unexpected future arrived before we'd finished with the past

These events are described as heart-breaking or heart-shattering. Something is shattered; we're torn apart and needing time and space to pull ourselves together for an unfamiliar future.

We're disillusioned. The illusion is gone.

The ego's addictions to form are shattered.

The ego is a fake self. Its control grows like a fungus in the darkness, feeding on illusions our minds have been taught to believe are success.

People *being* enlightened Presence, have the innate wisdom to know that Life's plan unfolds in seasons, and so we move through Life as humility, gratitude and peace.

Without Presence, we miss what's there now, thinking we'll get to it when we have less distractions and more time and money.

If we're not *being* Presence, we're missing Life as it's happening for us.

Loss re-minds us.

Loss awakens us to the fragile preciousness of Life. If we haven't brought Presence to our moments, disillusionment re-minds us that we're *being* what doesn't matter and that all of our materialistic stuff is the small stuff.

Gifts of Loss

As I write this I'm learning to find peace with a devastating new reality.

I'm living through a great loss and deepening my understanding of grief, chaos, Love and Presence.

This is my third morning since getting the phone call from a Canadian RCMP officer. He told me that my glorious floating home in its own cove in Canada's Coastal mountains, my beautiful sanctuary where I wrote much of this book, the place that I affectionately called my "Float Eden," had completely burned during the night.

I dearly and deeply loved everything about my sanctuary. Most of this book's ah-ha insights opened through me there.

Now I must surrender to the actions of greedy pirates, the hate crime henchmen who stole valuables and then obliterated my home.

Everything...family heirlooms, a lifetime of treasured gifts are all transformed.

I know that ego is attachment to form, however I can be nothing but sorrow now.

Being the impact of this, here in my friend's tiny guest room, I'm making a lonely journey through the depths of wounded despair.

It's a soul tsunami, and during today's most wretched moments of coming undone, I was swept to "the edge".

I peered into a dark swirling abyss of chaos. I felt its temptation to let go and plunge into its crazed, chaotic quandary of energy muck.

I was peering into chao's over-the-edge masquerade.

I could come undone and cross over to that dark side's realm of all-consuming anger, spitefulness, cruelty and greedy irresponsibility.

It would flip my heart's light inside out into a black hole.

There I could chuck my Presence into chaos and absolve myself of weighty responsibilities for pulling myself together and the climb back up to forgiveness and joy.

I could take an *over-the-edge* escape from returning to Love.

I could *be* beliefs that too much of Life is powerfully cruel, heartless, punishing and pointless. I could abandon Consciousness to be hate's chaos and cower—traumatized, invisable and silenced.

Well...that's not about to happen!

Hell no!

At that precipice of unbearable pain, I gathered all the Love I'd ever received, all the Love I'd ever been given. That Love is alive in me as me and I declared with ALL of my bruised BEing, "*I LOVE LOVING LIFE, EVEN NOW!*" With all of my energy I affirmed, "I LOVE LIFE".

"I LOVE BEING LIFE'S LIGHT!"
"I AM THAT LIGHT ALWAYS!"
"WE ARE ALL THAT LIGHT!"
I projected my Love and Light into that abyss of chaos and fear; there was a bright flash.
Its upsurge lifted me up...way up.
Where I was pure energy, freed of all pain.
Peace.

An awesome glorious goodness opened up. Possessions possess and I was free, really free to realize the whole planet is my home.
This is all so fresh and raw for me to be writing and putting into this book so soon.
I lived it. It happened.
The Grief of cruelty's soul-scalding wretchedness can take us out to *the edge*, beyond composure, to a chaos that inverts the Light of a human heart. Over that edge, we're transposed into unconscious, scrambling, light-sucking black holes.
I now understand the lowly energy realm of terrorists, tyrants, warlords, murderers and the greed-addicted.
They've gone over-the-edge, to being the scrambled, unconscious low life energy zone where smoldering chaos creeps and crawls.

Devastation Burns

As I process this new loss, the sanctuary of sleep is gone too. My nights have been torturous. Nightmare moments of the flames consuming each room and each piece of my sacred home, ignites my need to reach out to warn and protect—like a guardian to the endangered. What I'm going through feels like possible foreshadowing for our world.

There are pirates of peace that we've empowered.

Not long ago, anyone warning us of both the world-wide crisis of our environment, and deliberately orchestrated social and economic oppression, would have been considered a Chicken Little.

They would have been correct. We're witnessing the orchestrated collapses of both our globalized economy and our planet's ability to sustain nonviolent weather patterns.

Our societies and our planet need Life support, but economically, socially and environmentally most of us are doing more of the same, and hoping for a different outcome.

It has to get bad enough, for enough people to join the movement. How bad will it have to get for you? How at risk will your home need to be for you to *be* the change?

For a time, please feel what the months and years ahead will *be* if most of us stay apathetic.

Droughts have dried up vast areas. The weather gets more difficult and destructive and more nuclear radiation incidents have killed the ability of vast areas to support Life. Our safe places to *BE* are fewer, and our planet can't wrap any of us with easy comfort and safety. Too big to fail banks call the shots and year after year, the ongoing devastation of quality of Life for every species is unspeakable.

The climate crisis is already wiping out the ability of vast areas to provide coffee, chocolate, fruits, fish seafood and vegetables.

The Nov. 2011 warning from top international climate scientists and disaster experts was: Get ready for more dangerous and "unprecedented extreme weather".[1]

According to NASA, the National Center for Atmospheric Research and the National Oceanographic and Atmospheric Administration a destructive climate crisis is what's happening, but the powers that be do little to stop it.

Unstopped, the marauding agendas of the Illuminati and their executive pirates who rule the lands with globalization's bigness, corporatized media, militaries, oil addiction and shock and awe will continue to collapse quality of Life and our sense of *home*.

Depending on oil, money and banks to function gives *them* control over you.

Masses of us *being* the Presence of higher Consciousness is Life's greatest resource.

Presence lifts us above hatred and fear as it centers and harmonizes us.

IS-ness

When something changes everything, or when we feel unloved, unlucky, or unworthy, or when our dreams and future seem wrecked, consumed by the heat and flames of change, the future goes up in smoke and the ego can go into overdrive.

Trying to control, reason, force, deny and manipulate IS-ness back in line with your expectations is torturous.

Grief is the journey
from expectation
to peace with IS-ness.

When we're fighting to deny the IS-ness of reality, we're in a losing battle.

IS-ness is the truth and the power of Now.

Fighting to recover a past that doesn't exist stretches, warps and tears our Presence. It creates wretched pain.

This is why denial is, for a sane person, so uncomfortable to maintain.

No one who loves you wishes for you to be at war with Totality. Find your healthy balance of being an activist and surrendering to ISness.

When the destruction of maurading greed or extreme weather have impacted us, ego tries to make us the wounded, angry, stubborn, frightened and petty victim. These are the expected social steps of the control, loss, grieving, and recovery waltz.

Presence lifts us up.

There are great changes and losses ahead. You determine the level of Consciousness you return to after the grief.

Consciousness is like a rainbow of energies and at times we all drop down into fear and selfish doubt. No one who Loves you wants you to exist as hellishly low unconsciousness.

Our depths of dispair make angels weep.

Two Minute Healing

Opening Presence

When something changes everything, feel the space that is your awareness and open it.

Increase its spaciousness. Love it into opening and expanding.

Open your Consciousness and heart and mind to the peace of Now.

Our planet is still spinning around the Sun. Our whole solar system is cycling through our galaxy's torus with the ten billion other stars of our galaxy.

This is the grand galactic plan and you are part of its expanding consciousness.

Energy cannot be destroyed; it is only transformed. So let your pain be transformed into Love and expanding gratitude for what you've loved, and had. BE that Love, and allow your pain to go into your light of Consciousness. Allow the light of your *being* to transform your pain.

And then *BE* here Now, at peace with the new truths of Now.

This ends the painful trials of your mind, in which you are the accuser and accused, the judge, jury, witness, and victim.

Surrendering to the truth of Now returns peace to your *being*, and everyone who has ever loved you, throughout ALL of time, wishes this for you Now more than ever.

CHAPTER 8

Catharsis

The episodes and chapters of living are intended to be expanding and empowering, not impairing.

We humans are not designed to be putrid sponges for toxic emotions. We're designed to experience, learn the lessons, and use the contained energy pressures of dramas and traumas for enlightenment.

We're supposed to burn off the dross, the waste, dregs and scum of latent toxic emotions.

A great life is transformative! Nothing is intended to hang on for dear life or stay the same in the face of every thing's becoming.

Catharsis transforms the shadowy dungeons within us into the clear radiance of Consciousness.

Rather than running away from emotions or trying to bury or drug them into numbness, catharsis allows us to easily open them up and simply release their energy as fuel for *being*.

The Cathars

The Cathars were an enlightened and joyfully prosperous people who lived peacefully during the 11th to the 13th centuries in the Languedoc region of southern France.

They maintained a pure, energy-awareness of higher Consciousness and for more than ten generations, over two centuries, they embodied profound abilities to culture Consciousness.

Catharism was the name given to their ways.

Cathars connected with the pure spirit of Creation flowing through all things in all moments. They taught their children to *be* Oneness. We need only to remember photos of our Earth from our own moon to witness the truth of the Oneness we're living.

Their lives were peaceful, creative, beautiful and Loving celebrations, with a Life expectancy healthier and longer than in other regions of Europe.

They realized:

Life Loving Life creates Life.

Knowing that authentic Love does not coexist with a lust for ownership or control, they renounced all agendas of domination. [1]

Cathars had profoundly creative abilities, and their joyful celebration of Consciousness attracted many students. However the arts of Catharsis were destroyed because they threatened the agendas of conniving men addicted to wealth, power, and domination.

To the Cathars, Rome's opulent, aggressive and crusading government, disguised as church, represented the embodiment and manifestation of suppression, greed and evil.

The Catholic Church of Rome convinced French governors that the peaceful and prosperous Cathars were a threatening and growing mass movement. The Church launched the Albigensian Crusade to snuff out this enlightenment.

Many Cathar settlements were slaughtered without a fight; others passionately resisted.

In the end, the Albigensian Crusade (1209-1229) slaughtered an estimated one million people, both

Cathars and most of the sympathetic residents of Southern France.

When asked about the people living around the Cathar settlements and whether they should be spared, a pious leader of the crusade is famously quoted as saying: "Kill them all. God will recognize his own."

As I've been writing this, the Cathars and the Albigensian crusade have popped up in conversations half a dozen times, without my mentioning this chapter.

I've spoken with several people who connect deeply to the Cathars. The souls of those enlightened Cathars walk among us, alerting and awakening us.

The evolution of marches on Wall Street, and financial centers around our world, are the energy of the great social shift of our times. What began as an economic recession has revealed itself to be a globally humbling and healing shift of energies, an awakening leading to a renaissance.

Catharsis uses the Light of Consciousness to eliminate shadows of the past.

Life Is A Subtle Energy

Western nations can be clumsy and coarse when addressing subtle energies. We've clumped the black hole energies of the ego and the expansive high vibrations of Consciousness into one group and we've been taught to consider them all to be of one range of emotions.

To consider gratitude and Love to be of the same family of energies as greed and jealousy is naiveté.

The ego's black hole energies suck quality of experience and quality of Life into nothingness.

When we're *being* the expansiveness of forgiveness, hope, Love, Oneness, and gratitude (the Consciousness energies), we're a flowing, expansive Presence.

Consciousness and ego are very different presences.

Love creates, greed destroys.

Choose what you are *being* carefully.

The Pain Reservoir

We've been taught to contain, bury, judge, fear and chemically numb our accumulated emotions, and even to identify ourselves as our pain reservoir.

Containing the issues in our tissues has created health care industries and huge legal drug cartels, but not well-being.

The emotionally numbing drugs that unplug people from feelings, emotions and Presence do not eliminate repressed energies. Energy is designed to move, and when blocked, old toxic emotions corkscrew inward.

The heavy, downhearted emotions that we gather and dam into the pain reservoir become toxic, festering energies from which the ego feeds. The root of the word damage is to dam, to block flow. We have millions of damned people struggling to contain toxic, repressed emotional baggage.

For people who feel like toxic waste dumps of old emotions and chemicals, a natural way to flow and grow has arrived.

Through Catharsis we discover the fuel for Consciousness IS the pain we transform. Heavy hearted emotions can be the fuel of enlightenment.

The Art of Catharsis

Catharsis transforms dark, low-vibrational fearful emotions, the toxic output of an impulsive, compulsive brain and a fearful egoic mind. Catharsis releases the dark tightness and trauma in your body, so healing energies can flow through and cleanse you physically.

Light transforms darkness.

Light penetrates, transforms and energizes darkness.

Catharsis transforms old deadweight emotions like a fire burns off dry, old wood. What was dead and collapsing, becomes light, warm expansive energies.

Just as the waves of energy radiating from a light bulb illuminate darkness, your inner light of Consciousness transforms dark, dead weight emotions into the Light of Life.

When a great cosmic star exhausts its fuel source, it collapses into its own gravity. It becomes an energy and light sucking void of intense density.

Ego fueled by the intense voids of fear, greed and addictions is a black hole to well-being. No matter how much ego-feeding attention and things a greed-addicted person gets, there is never enough.

Catharsis transforms darkness and chaos into Light.

Cathartic Cleansing

Feelings are energy, and energy is designed to move!

Emotions move in one of three ways:

- They corkscrew into our body's pain reservoir. Many emotion-blocking drugs direct this process.

- They move out into the environment through the voice, crying, laughing, physical movement, forgiveness, Loving or creative endeavors.

- They are enlightened through catharsis to fuel the Light of Consciousness.

Catharsis is our highest calling. Each of us can be a cleanser of the heavy sludge, the deadly emotional baggage that weighs down our spirits and our planet. Each of us can shine as The Light.

Rather than containing or stuffing feelings, catharsis allows us to open an internalized energy like a blossom, to receive its lesson if there is one, and then to allow the emotion to fuel Consciousness. With the healing that follows you'll experience pain dissipating.

Allow old toxic emotions to go into your Consciousness, and become fuel for your inner light.

A strengthened liberated, sustainable well-being follows.

If you have habitually identified yourself as your suffering and victimhood, catharsis requires courage. It takes practice and sometimes feels counterintuitive.

Society has taught us to judge, fear, avoid and bury feelings. We've been taught to identify with our pain reservoir, rather than to empty and transform it.

Catharsis returns us to our individual capacity to be energy purifiers, creators, lovers, and contributors to Creation Consciousness.

Catharsis requires focus and several steps.

The Cathartic Healing
Catharsis

The steps are outlined here. You might make your own audio recording that you can pause, or have a generous of spirit, trusted friend or group leader read through this as you follow the steps.

If you have someone reading through it, set up a signal, like the lifting of a finger, that indicates you're ready to move to the next step. You can also experience this with me by listening to the Catharsis audio program at consciousworldsummit.com.

Sit or lie comfortably.

With the essence your being strongly, silently affirm that you are Light and that heavy, dark or lost energies have no place within you.

Feel the life energies within you and fill yourself with gratitude for the possibility of this moment. Let the gratitude open and fully *be* expansive gratitude.

You feel gratitude through your awareness. Allow that awareness to open, expand and enlighten, and then fully *be* that Consciousness.

Search through your body, brain and mind to find the old issues in your tissues, the blockages and pain reservoirs. Find the painful, heavy or dark energies.

What color, temperature or qualities do these heavy, dark energies have?

Now move your awareness to an area of your body that is calm, flowing, open and at ease. What color, temperature or energy does this clear and flowing place have?

Now move through your *being* and let the heavy dark energies flow into your inner light of Consciousness.

The old toxic pain is not you; it is not your badge for living, your identity, or your purpose. It's just heavy, chaotic, sludge energy that pulls you and everything down.

Move your awareness to each of the heavy energy areas where the old, toxic pain, tightness, blockages and heaviness are. They needn't be a part of you any more.

In each area, allow the pain space to open and expand. If it has a lesson, allow its wisdom to easily fill your awareness. And then gratefully let the color and energies of old toxic heaviness go into your own inner light, like fuel to a fire.

Let all the dramas and traumas of the past be fuel for your BEing.

To Love Loving Life is the fuel for expanding Consciousness. Let go and let the light of your Presence now in this moment, absorb the past.

And then simply *BE* Presence.

Allow your Presence of Consciousness to bathe all the areas that used to harbor pain, with healing, flowing Light.

Where the pain used to be, hold the Presence of Consciousness from this time forward.

Fill yourself with the expanding Light of your Consciousness and hold that as your authentic *being*.

This is your authentic eternal Presence of BEing.

Creation is everywhere in everything, *BE*ing this moment now. Open up your Consciousness, expand it to be one with all of this moment now.

All we ever have is the Presence of Now and you have arrived for it.

With a bit of practice and trust you'll experience tremendous cathartic cleansing. You'll be able to let go of coping mechanisms that crept into your life, to wrangle the wretchedness from your old pain reservoir. You'll be able to trust and Love yourself.

Each time you use catharsis, you're a cleansing Presence, rather than a toxic holding tank.

When we transform heavy, toxic emotions we rid our Earth of heavy energies.

Share this process with yourself and others generously.

Sexual Catharsis

Aristocracies, addicted to controlling through suppression, taught us to feel alienated and separated from Creation. For centuries they've considered the dumbed down masses to be asses.

They turned guilt and shame along with superiority of race, religion, nationality and class into franchised religiosity. To humiliate, control and shame, they arrogantly taught us that *being* a human involved something base, dirty and dark— and that sexuality was our own tempting, tainted, guilty darkness. And for guilt-riddled, war-torn centuries of slavery and desperation, the oppressed masses bought in.

Let's simply look at the energetic truth. We are in electrical and magnetic bodies on an electrical and magnetic planet, ALL relying on energy, friction and heat to exist. For health and well-being, we need to be grounded in our bodies, to the Earth and to Loving Life. As adults we need spirit liberating lightening bolts of energy-aligning orgasms.

In the same way that we can't have healthy crops without lightening strikes that electrify the soil and release fresh batches of nitrogen, we humans naturally and holistically need body, mind and Consciousness expanding cosmic orgasms.

I'm talking about reaching a heightened cathartic bliss that leaves the planet's third dimensionality and opens up our very *BE*ings to blow the boxes off our minds, hearts and bodies so that we expansively float–and are one with a high plateau of Cosmic Consciousness.

There we arrive to glimpse and to be healed by the higher dimensions.

Take a moment to recall a most delicious and satisfying meal–something that stays with you as a supremely peak experience.

A Cosmic Orgasm is the meal you've just remembered, as compared to a paper bag of cold fast food.

Fast food equates to the quality of the sexual experiences of people with guilty, ashamed, dirty-little-closed-minds. Their sexuality is not centered in higher Consciousness and isn't healing or transcendent.

To achieve any orgasm we need to focus our mind and open to *being* a dreamy energy state. For a cosmic orgasm we open up our Presence of higher Consciousness and let go of the self to *BE* the lightening that expansively, explosively unites with ALL.

You must *BE* Presence to win!

A cosmic orgasm is the magic carpet ride of lore, the ride to a transcendent energy plateau of multidimensional expansiveness.

You are the ongoing expanding energy of *The Big Bang* and responsible, safe sex centered in Love is your ticket to ride.

Let go and Bang BIG!

The End of Shame for BEing

Humans are the only species to exhibit shame and guilt for simply *being*. We're the only species to teach shame for existing, the only species that believes that there's something else, some other plan or place that's infinitely better than now. All the Universe's creative energies and potentials are right there where you are.

This whole world is an orchestrated orgasmic orgy of *beingness*, isn't it?

When we allow our physical abilities to reach up through energy planes, to arrive at and glimpse Totality from the peaks of Cosmic Orgasms and then to let go, what we bring back to Earth is something beyond Love.

We bring Universal Consciousness.

We are the ongoing happening and expansion of *The Big Bang*.

Love's Magic Carpet Ride

More than ever, we need to be conscious, careful, responsible and safe with our sexuality.

Sexuality is not designed to be squandered or bartered. We need to hold this ability to journey energetically, and to *be* lightening bolts of clarifying energy, with a sacred regard.

Presence fuels the chemistry of relationships, it's the alchemy of the magic carpet ride of Love and sensuality.

*BE*ing the Presence of higher Consciousness is your ticket to orgasmically "leave the planet" and ride the Light fantastic.

We have to get over ourselves to fully *BE*!

Liberation of Consciousness

Regimes, monarchies and religions taught us, time after historic time, to be shame-based. They made us believe that we regular folks have been cast out, alienated from Creation's graces.

From childhood, they corrupted our Consciousness by teaching us that we <u>must</u> court the grace of God by serving those bejeweled, gold robed princes of greed-addicted political aristocracies—and their smug, scary faith franchisers in their gilded palaces.

They taught us to have a shame-based, guilty relationship with *being* and too often that we're the sexually filthy playground of a devil.

Meanwhile history shows us that more of us were slaughtered in their greedy holy wars than by famines, natural disasters and plagues combined.

Perhaps greed is the ultimate plague.

What if shame and greed's hypocritical and schizophrenic approach to *being, is* the bleeding wound of our heartbreaks? What if the empty lostness at the center of our *beings* is confusion, frustration and guilt because we've believed that we're expelled from God's heart? What if that has turned us into centuries of needy, greedy, competing and comparing, dumbed down, unconscious combatants?

A heart trying to Love Life through an emotional reservoir of fear, alienation, judgments, prejudice, pain and bitter disappointment is mired in toxic energies and therefore quick to fear, accuse, defend and attack. And that's how we've been carefully taught to *be* for many centuries.

What if feeling separated and cast out from Creation's heart is the forbidden apple in our Planetary Garden of Eden, and the serpents of our story are the teachers and franchisers of guilt, shame and hate?

That old paradigm is collapsing into its own hypocrisy and greed.

All of the Universe's energies and higher Consciousness are right there, composing you and everything around you now.

Everything is energy! The higher realms of Consciousness and Creation's flow and grace opens freely for us all. Higher Consciousness liberates us all from low energy prisons of the mind, and we needn't tithe to anyone to get the keys to freedom.

Your free will's ability to chose the energy you're *BE*ing is your key.

What if Life is simple?

The truth is we really don't need much to be joyfully happy with the beauty of a day.

According to international surveys of happiness, possessing less creates more freedom and happiness. Staying out of debt appears to be the way to easy happiness?

Perhaps the collapse of the old greedy economy is our awakening from a big bad dream?

The age has arrived for us to free ourselves from the tyranny of greed and to expose the Wizards of our Oz, ruling the lands with bigness, greed and debt.

The collapses of toxic old institutions, the government bankruptcies and the fall and decline of uncivilization is our liberation!

We are the generations launching The Renaissance of Consciousness. It's a new age, when we gather with our local Communities of Consciousness, to more simply and joyfully Love Loving Life. Our Loving hearts' desires are opening up a higher, more beautiful and expansive realm of *being*. This is our era to really Love Loving Life without shame or guilt for *being* human.

The enlightenment of your Consciousness is your key.

When you honor, Love and whole-heartedly cherish your Life, you don't long for someone else to do it for you.

Blossom your essence, the higher consciousness in your mind and your heart and give yourself your own approval, your own Love, so it fills you with Life's radiant glow. Give Love and gratitude to your *being* and exceptionally beautiful happenings will flow to you and through you.

Love isn't a word, it's *BE*ing the energy.

BEing Social Catharsis

Let's learn from worthy teachers of liberation.

Martin Luther King, Jr. was greatly inspired by India's Mahatma Gandhi, whose mission was to non-violently create freedom through the restoration of India's Consciousness.

Gandhi's teachings have a resounding resiliency. Most people of Bangladesh have virtually no material wealth; however they are consistently rated among the happiest people in the world.

Meanwhile, people with the highest standards of living (and the most needy expectations) are rated the unhappiest.

Dr. King traveled to India and said about Gandhi, "He was probably the first person in history to lift the Love ethic of Jesus above mere interaction between individuals to an effective social force on such a large scale."

"Do to others as you would have them do to you."
Jesus, Luke 6.31

"Consider others as yourself."
Buddha, Dhammapada 10.1

This awareness—spoken by teachers separated by three thousand miles, languages, two drastically different cultures and five hundred years—flow from the same high Consciousness that heals people and nations time after time.

Throughout the New Testament and ancient Buddhist scriptures, we discover that the lives, values, deeds and teachings of Jesus and Buddha, are the harmonious instruments, lyrics and music of our Universe—the song of Creation's Oneness.

Your free will is to liberate yourself from idolizing mere words, and to feel and fully *BE* the realm of Consciousness that great teachers embody and offer their lives up to. This higher Consciousness is the authentic Presence that is the heartbeat of empathy, compassion, caring and sharing.

The lasting reward of higher Consciousness is the beginning of sustainable happiness Now.

Teachers of Consciousness speak in the present tense.

Gandhi and Dr. King connected us to the Presence and to the peacefully creative possibilities of higher Consciousness here and now.

Gandhi and Dr. King used that Presence to create an awakening that eventually healed nations perpetually wounded by the prejudice, judgment, and terrorism of low Consciousness.

Now we call upon it to heal our entire planet.

Quality of Consciousness determines quality of experience for ALL.

But Why?

Why would Creation put Consciousness into bodies in the first place?

Why dinosaurs and then humans?

Life is energy made brilliant!

Through Life, the pure energy of Creation manifesting as Consciousness is expanding and evolving to be more of itself. Creation is still becoming, and we are Creation's possibility!

True, it may sometimes feel as if we are Creation's Saturday morning cartoon, but the ways that Life's beauty flows are very simple.

Love Loves Love,

Hope Loves Hope,

Being Loves *Being*,

so that Life Loves Life.

But hatred does not Love hatred. Even haters long to be Loved. They just don't know how to create the real thing yet.

There, on the very soil where Jesus Christ taught us to *BE* Love, hate still taints the whole place. This hate puts us all at great risk.

Some great lessons require great loss.

After the dust has settled, we will learn to *BE* Love Loving Life.

A festival is much more fun than a smoldering dead zone or black hole.

Christ Consciousness is the pure Presence of Creation's Consciousness—the pilot light of our hearts.

Love Life and abundantly share it.

Peace is that simple!

Lift yourself off these mere words and open your mind, your heart, and then your whole *being* and feel the Life energy that is you!

Do this now and Love Loving your own *being*.
Feel the Life energy flowing through your body.
Feel that energy, radiating as the Light beyond
light within you and radiating out from you, and
give it more room to expand and to flow and grow.
  BE the LIGHT!
  Open to LIFE just as it is now.
  Please just BE LIFE's Loving flow with the next
few moments and you will experience another
form of catharsis.

Love your Love
of what you LOVE
and wish this
same joy for everyone!

Do this whenever, wherever, and however you
are, and you're home!

Two Minute Healing

What Doesn't Matter

Imagine for a couple of full minutes that you are
an angel of Light, liberated from gravity's grip.
Imagine you're looking down at your self, living
Life here on Earth.
  As pure spirit/consciousness, what are you
telling your self?
  Listen for the message to come through you.

CHAPTER 9

Achievement Strategies

One way or another, we've all learned achievement strategies—ways to make things happen and get things done. These strategies are born from paradigms, sets of beliefs about how life works. All organizations, businesses, and professions have an achievement strategy in play.

Sharks, Dolphins and Turtles

With a nod to Dudley Lynch and Paul L. Kordis's *Strategy of the Dolphin*, let's look at achievement strategies from the perspective of higher consciousness.

Sharks

Shark personalities are voraciously unconscious users and consumers—for them, enough isn't enough, and more of everything is a necessity.

They experience a day as an ego-driven, shark-eat-shark, everyone-for-themselves, I've-got-to-get-mine-before-someone-else-does battleground. They have a fundamental belief in scarcity—that there can't possibly be enough to comfortably go around.

Their everyday language tends to use war terminology like, "battle plan," "dropped a bombshell," "war room," "heavy artillery," "good soldier," "battlefront"...

Shark personalities around the world were raised from childhood to never be fulfilled or contented. Competitive, comparative and egoic, they've suffered burning humiliations. They grow up to be hostile, low consciousness, opportunistic, dark-hearted, sore losers addicted to comparing and competing, resorting to any means to feed their unappeasable egos. They'll use fear, intimidation, humiliation, terrorism, brute-strength, force, chaos, spin, cheating and trickery to feed their ego addictions to winning and status.

Desperate for the admiration of their race, company, sect, faction, religion, cult, denomination, troop, tribe, gang, or splinter group, they experience themselves as an internal void.

Sharks don't have an open relationship with the Consciousness of the heart. Their hearts were encased in protective armor long ago.

Every group is a splinter group.

One shark achievement strategy is to rile groups of people up by creating a frenzy of confusion, shock, awe and chaos. While everyone is topsy-turvy, sharks step to center stage and calmly tell the panicked masses what needs to happen next.

When orders have been carried out, sharks turn down the chaos so it simmers just enough for people to stay disturbed and obediently afraid.

Sharks are addictive and greedy. They leverage loyalty to "our righteous cause" to justify doing whatever it takes to win. For a shark, being *in* control means constantly being *on* patrol.

Their life is a hunt, and they've convinced themselves they love the kill. Bloodthirsty, they strategically muzzle, sacrifice, or exile voices that threaten their agendas.

Sharks are addicted, close-minded loners with few loyalties.

Egoic sharks stick to old-school industrial-militarization paradigms of waging wars, brute force or to obedient, low consciousness soldiering.

When a case is made for reinventing or not reinventing, sharks get busy stirring the pot of reasons to manage change by doing more of the same more intensely.

Aristocratic sharks are the greed-addicted 1% that groups as shadow governments and shareholders that threaten, humiliate and terrorize their debt-enslaved approval-addicted worker-sharks. Alien to grass-roots values, opinions in coffee shops and subtle shifts in concern and confidence, they won't be inventing solutions that will rejuvenate and sustain mothers, fathers, their children, or our environment.

To elite sharks, an educated middle-class is troublesome and needs to shrink. Their industrial age, wool-over-their-eyes blinders block Consciousness and Oneness with ALL, keeping them defensively ignorant of reality, people, the environment, climates, trends and the values of higher Consciousness.

They discount criticism because they consider critics to be jealous. When a shark hasn't initiated a plan, they consider it an enemy.

They believe what their minds have already closed in on. Denial is a shark's dark den.

The shark-mind expects the future to mirror the past, but it never does. Most sniffing dogs have more consciousness of the subtle energies of character, agenda and change than egocentric sharks who bank on future scenarios obediently accommodating their five-year-plans.

As change marches onward, sharks use politicized clout to make their militaristic "defense" strategies stick—so they alone will stay on top, rather than allowing all of us to thrive collectively.

Most sharks are afraid, wounded and hurting—they're increasingly lost and baffled by this decline and fall of extremist capitalistic-militarism.

I'm convinced that some sharks are so voraciously addicted to getting more, that they're addicted to addiction! They believe the doctrines so much that they can't begin to fathom how to simply and peacefully *be* enough.

Sharks don't know how to arrive at bliss by simply slowing down and *being* the full, peaceful presence of higher Consciousness.

They need transformational compassion. Sharks need relearning opportunities to experience how Consciousness fills the wretched void that white-knuckle addicts endure.

Dolphins

Dolphin personalities embody a playful open-hearted generosity of spirit.

They believe our planet is capable of shared, simple abundance. They're popular, open-minded learners who creatively think outside the box.

Dolphins sense the flow see trends of change, and courageously attune us all to these new patterns and paradigms.

As leaders, they strive to create the highest, sustainable good for ALL. They tend to have long tenures as managers and leaders because they're generous-of-spirit team players. They're accomplishment-oriented people who know that only a mutually-beneficial clean win is a true and lasting win.

Dolphins are good listeners and passionate learners. They're engaging, aware, resourceful, balanced, evolving Consciousness. They know we must creatively, resourcefully, and consciously *be* the initiative of sustainable solutions.

Dolphin personalities are teachers for our Communities of Consciousness.

Turtles

Humans with turtle achievement strategies don't trust themselves or their talents. The pressures of making a choice can make turtle personalities physically ill.

Afraid of risk, their primary loyalty is to safety-through-sameness.

Sharks often populate committees with turtles because they're excellent "yes" people who've learned that being front and center puts them at risk for humiliation. As children, turtles learned to be seen and not heard; they learned to be silent until called upon.

In nature, some species of turtles have even developed the ability to keep their head in the sand while they breathe through their asses.

Slow-moving turtles resent talent and fear being left behind by those disturbingly innovative dolphins.

Turtles are sometimes passive-aggressive. Snapping turtles, while appearing harmless, sabotage new dolphin created solutions just because managing change requires courage and talent. As members of committees, they'll often wait until a decision is about to be made, then they'll release a key piece of information they've been holding back. Thus, through chaos, they passive-aggressively wield influence by returning everyone to square one.

An environment of action or turbulence sends turtles cowering back into their shells where they keep a low-profile until it's safe to come out. After a clear winner has been declared, they cozy up and follow that leader.

If conditions aren't clear and sunny, turtles hide down in the muck.

Many turtles repeatedly follow a sick script that casts them as the losers or victims in relationships and endeavors.

Government bureaucracies, and the offices of billionaires, are havens for colonies of turtles.

Politically powerful sharks surround themselves with turtles. When the sharks are exposed as man eaters, turtles with plea bargains can discover their sunniest days can be spent whistle blowing.

As schools of dolphins trust being the higher Consciousness that creates Life's sustainable solutions, turtles will eventually stick their necks out, stop breathing through their asses, and join Life's renaissance.

The Very Best At Humility

The shark said to the turtle, "This product is going to be huge! Everybody will want it...except those environmentalists."

The turtle listened with rapt awe as the strutting shark proclaimed, "This will make us bloody rich! People won't be able to get enough of it, the chemists made sure of that. And then you know what we're going to need to be?"

"No. What?", inquired the shy turtle.

"We're going to need to be folksy, so we don't attract too much attention. We're going to need to be the very best at humility!"

"Humble!", proclaimed the turtle. "I can do that!"

"Yes", mused the shark, "To stay under the radar we'll need to pride ourselves on our humility! And that's why you, my turtle friend, are perfect for the job of my Director of Public Relations!"

You Buy Your Ticket
You Take The Ride

On a carnival midway you buy your ticket, and you take the ride—if you see people turned upside down, that ride will topsy-turvy you, too.

Sharks try to convince their turtle followers that topsy-turvy won't happen to us, "because you're with me and we're *the* chosen people".

Sharks hire on-the-take scientists and economists to convince us that unconscious greed does not cause our planet's pneumonia, weak economies, foreclosures, unemployment, choking debt, despair, or the collapse of civilizations.

Regardless of lessons, patterns and cycles of human history, sharks are too greed-addicted, doctrine following and blood thirsty to realize that history repeats itself because sharks repeat history.

They repeat the sins of the fathers by being so above-it-all, they don't take the same ride as *the common folk.*

Executives and upper-management too often get perked out of their own product's marketplace. Their families are no longer after-tax consumers because their product is a free perk of executive entitlement. This ends truthful intimacy with the product's consciousness, value and the whole buyer/user experience.

Among executives of big automakers, how many have personally paid for a car in the past fifteen years? Has anyone in their immediate families borrowed money to buy a car?

Probably not.

Top management hires consultants who go to the mall and come back to report what's happening. Salespeople, who know the customer experience are undervalued and exiled from that echelon.

Conscious commerce puts management and leadership right there, face-to-face, with their community's consumer experience. Community rapport is a requirement for sustainability.

Money's New Paradigm

As exchanges, barter and trade grow, money is less important. When climactic military and climatic Earth events happen, we'll pay more attention to tangibles that satisfy essential needs.

We'll see that devalued money doesn't make the world go around or Life happen. Nature, water, weather, green growth, community, Consciousness and Creation's Love of Life are what makes Life flow.

We got our tickets, and we're taking the ride.

Consciousness is our ticket to ride.

The skill-set and Consciousness of the dolphins will usher us into the next age for humanity.

Meanwhile those sharks...

Shark personalities, particularly in oil and in the industrial-military complex, amassed monstrous wealth early in the new millennium.

Bloodthirsty sharks, addicted to fear-fueled militarized capitalism, will continue fixating on promising different results by doing more of the same.

Even during hurricane-force winds of change, sharks and their flocks of turtle-followers will cling to carefully selected religious sound-bites to justify an ignorance that says, "Don't confuse me with your science or journalistic research. I don't trust new facts. Research can be wrong! I know what I know. Full steam ahead with more of the same."

The winds of change reveal the truth like a frigid autumn wind strips naked a tree.

Truth backs know-it-all sharks into the corners of their boxed, closed minds. Rather than humbly observe and learn, they'll stubbornly stick to their guns, determined to accomplish different goals by doing more of the same at twice the velocity. This pattern defines *insanity*.

Being the low consciousness of ego gets us into challenging situations in which we think, "What am I going to do? How am I going to get past this without anyone knowing that I'm scared and that I don't know what to do, and can't admit it?"

Sharks live with the inner hollowness of fear, hiding what they *don't* know behind tradition, institutions, religiosity, smoke and mirrors, false bravado, threats, and militaristic muscle.

Sharks are addicted to the old-school's old-paradigm beliefs and, like all unconscious addicts, they will need to hit bottom with a bang, before seeing stars and the Light of Consciousness.

Humans have loved to layer complicating cultures around essential truths and cultures are not designed to shrink themselves. Cultures are designed to sustain, grow and embellish themselves; however any culture or system driven hard, to its extremities, soon self-destructs.

It's up to the dolphins to convince masses of turtles that we're awakening a new paradigm, a new holistic, balanced approach to being sustainable Life.

Simple truths needn't be lacquered, enrobed in threads of gold or reinforced by statues of stone. The energy and how it flows is the simple truth and that's all we need to teach and be.

As corrupted institutions of greed collapse, the opportunity of the dolphins is to compassionately teach the turtles that we each peacefully and safely co-create global mass Consciousness every day with what we buy and what we peacefully stand for together.

When we stop buying from and funding those sharks, they'll change.

The old adage, "He who has the gold rules" is true only if our mass Consciousness remains beguiled and addicted to that gold.

He who has the gold rules
only as long as we value
quantity of wealth
more than quality of Life.

Our mass addiction to worshipping money and brands led some western nations to borrow to bail-out greed-addicted shark-bankers. The usurious lenders who do in others as they do unto others.

usury | ˈyoō zh (ə)rē | noun
Lending money at unreasonably high rates of interest.

Early in the agricultural economy con artists, usurers who tricked, violated and crushed hard working people and their families, would be humiliated and walked to the county line. After this "walk of shame" they were told never to return.

Not long ago, today's big banks, credit card companies and unscrupulous lenders would have been marched out of town and into prisons. Usury lending used to be illegal.

His campaign to expose usurious lenders is what we're told Jesus Christ died for.

Only an addictive low-consciousness society would borrow to bail out Wall Street, Fred and Fanny and other lenders and their wicked ways with little or no financial accountability or justice.

If you had a bowl of cocaine and you carried it into a group of addicts, you'd be amazed at how quickly that cocaine disappeared. If you asked where it all went, nobody would quite know. But very soon they'd be begging for more.

Money is our cocaine.

The executive pirates, their henchmen economists and shareholders addicted to exponential growth, the shopaholics and debt-choked hyper-consumers are addicts too.

We're all in withdrawal.

We've been addicted to beliefs that money creates happiness, security and well-being, and that more money means more happiness.

We've had a mass global economic meltdown. It's addicts hitting bottom and we're living through an after-binge ratcheting down of our conspicuous consumption.

In the sobering fall of 2008, masses of people shifted from buying their feelings to simply *being* the feelings they desire. And since that turning point, conscious people are more aware of *what doesn't matter.*

We're more conscious.

The earlier bubbling U.S. economy was a Ponzi scheme playing out in the global unconsciousness.

It was a scheme based on Americans buying things with no way of paying for them. The U.S. became a debt-based economy. With offshore oil dependancies and the hemorrhaging of multiple shark infested wars, there couldn't be enough U.S. dollars to back the inflated values.

Money was no longer tied to anything more tangible than perceptions, imagined values and numbers on a screen. We were flying high like careening, intoxicated addicts until...

Crash!

As institutions, brands, and faith collapsed into black holes of greed, the mass Consciousness shifted. It happened suddenly.

We simply stopped spending.

The allure shopping malls used to have, the glitz, suddenly looked and felt hollow and cheap—like dark, boozy discotheques the morning after.

A hangover has to be bleak enough, black enough and painful enough for addicts to snap out of their addictions.

People will endure the pain of withdrawal, and the loneliness of releasing the old cultures, to move from a place of pain up to a place they trust will stay less painful.

We're in a mass addiction recovery program.

Things got bad enough and thanks to the marches shedding light on greed around the world, we're snapping out of it.

The marches on Wall Street and greed around the world are a mass addiction intervention. One of the messages may need to be for Moms and Dads to stop mortgaging Life's future by financing the 1%. We need to rejuvenate our local economies in every way we can.

A shout out needs to be for Dolphins, turtles, and yes, even stock-ticker shocked sharks to stop unconsciously gobbling-up what sloppy bigger-business, usurious lenders and oil-thirsty militarism have been dishing out.

Hope does not grow if we try to get ahead by going backwards. Our solution isn't more jobs in corporations that stratify wealth out of local economies and up to the 1%.

Hope grows by moving forward, up through the lightness of higher Consciousness.

Let the universal wisdom of a loving mother's hopes for her child's future, in her family's local community, light the path.

Regain Consciousness and stand up for Life! Stand up for Life in board rooms, conference rooms and the other chambers of the wizards of our Oz. Stand for Life in the checkout lines of the stores with what you choose to support. March with the agents of change, demonstrate the changes your local community needs itself to create.

Now in this moment, as this moment, you contribute and draw from a mass Consciousness on the move. We track aspects of it with consumer confidence.

We won't grow sustainable consumer confidence if, in our hearts, we know that what we're consuming dooms us?

Consuming what the greed-addicted 1% dishes out dooms life. Let's rejuvenate local economies in green ways, so we're unfettered and alive!

A Foreclosure On Greed

With the dawn of this new millennium, a few hundred greed-addicted banker-sharks perpetrated history's grandest mismanagement and usury violations against humanity. It's an economic perfect storm foreclosing on the dark ages of unconscious business practices.

Our thinking has changed and survival is centering itself. It makes no sense to blame, and then asking to be rescued by, big greedy business.

As the great global shift continues, caring for our local communities and our whole Earth centers our thoughts and values more than occupying a corporate occupation.

The higher Consciousness of loving grandmothers, mothers and enlightened open-minded, open-hearted men everywhere are hope's greatest hope.

Hear your heart's call from Creation. Look into the eyes of people in uniforms and tell them never to turn their weapons on innocent civilians.

Buy local and support conscious commerce and green businesses and celebrate your local solutions.

BE what you're for! Support, celebrate and recommend good local business.

March into City Hall and teach them to be business friendly to local entrepreneurs rather than malls. Grow your region's Community of Consciousness and green economy, so we leave the big bad brands wondering how we all suddenly got so smart.

Soon we'll be opening our eyes in the mornings to see a much more beautiful community and world.

Take some time to feel how beautiful that will feel every day.

CHAPTER 10

Our New Economy

*T*he newly deceased's Consciousness was
asked, *"Why were you not fully alive?"*

"What? What do you mean?" the confused

man asked.

"Why were you not joyfully and lovingly alive?"

"I was afraid of being embarrassed," the

confused man answered.

"But the shame you felt all your adult life was

your embarrassment for not Loving Life."

"Oh", said the man, "is that what that was?"

"I was afraid", is not going to be an adequate
excuse.

The old shark-eat-shark rules of big-business
industrial pirates don't work now.

Greed collapses energies and Consciousness
creatively expands them.

So bring it!

If you don't bring your Consciousness into this
life, you'll have done little of lasting value.

The scientific research of Dr. Konstantin
Korotkov backs this up.

He has seen how gratitude and Love expand and activate space in beautiful ways, and how greed creates chaos in the entropy of space.

He has witnessed this at micro levels and he articulately attributes it to broader social events.

"I was born in The Soviet Union," he says. "We saw institutions collapse in a short period of time, gone like a mist, because it was an evil empire against the individual, against originality and various forms of higher Consciousness.

"Consciousness and collective Consciousness is the transforming force of human history. A lot of things are happening just now. We are living in a very active time politically, socially and environmentally. Now we are transforming to a new type of this Consciousness. It is a huge movement in the world.

"With the new society that is developing, this marriage of science, technology, religion, spirituality will be absolutely natural, integrated so we can overcome all the developmental divisions that were created in the 18th and 19th centuries.

"In the new society, Consciousness and spirituality will be the emotional center of human beings.

"People who work hard, have talent and new ideas, bright minds of high Consciousness, will find great acceptance and successes."

Conscious Commerce

Awakenings, rejuvenation and transformation are born through crisis.

Not getting what you thought you wanted is often the kiss of greater good luck.

Conscious commerce opens through sensibilities deep within us and then blossoms out as wisdom, awareness, values, choices and actions. It expands out through family, community, the Internet, the media, the mass Consciousness, into the meetings of conscious organizations, the stores, the schools, and eventually into political/ military agendas.

Beliefs are the stories that comfort. Stories, beliefs, paradigms and possibilities are being rewritten now.

The wizards of our OZs, who built great monumental towers with lobbies designed to intimidate and silence mere *people*, haven't been thinking on a human or natural scale for quite some time. They look, think, dress, evaluate and act on corporate and governmental scales. They're too often out of touch with Life.

Conscious commerce is built on family and community scales. They're relationship-centered enterprises that honor, comfort, include and nurture us, rather than intimidate, baffle and silence us.

Conscious people are using this global shift, these teachable moments, to pause, regain Consciousness and liberate our future.

Our new economy invites us to shake free from institutionalized left-brain linear obsessions to the more holistic, pattern-visioning, quality-of-life and artistic possibilities of right-brain creativity.

What Daniel Pink encouraged in his book, *A Whole New Mind: Why Right-Brainers Will Rule The Future* (Riverhead Books, 2006) is definitely a step in the—please pardon the pun—right direction.

Reinvention and rejuvenation require the right-brain's creative pattern, change and trend awareness.

We are now BEing the greatest social shift and business reinvention of our generations—old aristocracy-worshipping rules, socially etched into our brains, aren't birthing our new economy's sustainable solutions—local heros are.

A medical triage is assigning degrees of urgency to wounds or illnesses and deciding the order of treatment of a large number of patients or casualties.

As we triage our way into our future, we're discovering that quality of life flows through quality of consciousness and we're forming new kinds of complimentary communities like never before.

It's high time for higher Consciousness.

Our Earth is contracting a global pneumonia, so Life on Earth is in triage mode too.

> Sustainability grows through respectful interrelationships of people, Nature and community.

Our rejuvenation opportunities are born through regional green economies that create or use clean, affordable energy innovations.

Addictions to dirty energy are our problem. Clean, simple and efficient energy innovations, that can be used by emerging economies everywhere, are our solutions.

From Wall to Main Streets

When stocks took a dive in 2008-09 and the values of big brands were down, the Chinese went shopping and also became the lenders for sinking-ship business and panic-ridden government bailouts.

The Chinese government quietly gained influence and profit positioning within American corporations as they also took over many powerful U.S. law firms.

When we wonder what's next for the U.S., we need to take an honest look at how the U.S. treated other countries over which it gained economic influence and then factor in Chinese values and agendas and consciousness.

The fact that big brands are increasingly owned and influenced by mysterious off-shore entities opens the way for more home-grown, relationship-centered, regional green solutions.

We're migrating from unconscious loyalties to big brands with bad reputations, to efficiency-driven innovations and solutions created by people we can personally know and trust. Their homespun branding communicates, "We're lean, green and locally seen."

Each American spending just $3.33 annually for made in the USA products, creates 10,000 new jobs. Buy locally created products and you'll see the economy you live in rejuvenate.

New economic "communities" are taking many creative forms. Green and conscious co-ops and intentional communities are springing up everywhere, on and off-the-grid.

These communities flip us from competing, comparing and keeping-up-with-the-Joneses to being cooperative. Both nuclear and chosen families live, co-create, share the harvest and weather the storms together.

Living simply, while supporting conscious commerce, lifts us above dog-eat-dog business and its fraying of the quality and environmental fabric of Life.

The great global shift is redefining wealth as freedom from the tyranny of greed-addicted sharks. By no longer being pawns in their toxic chess game, we're saving Life one community at a time.

What was the dollar-driven and greed-addicted mainstream is receding into an antiquated fringe, and what was fringe is blossoming as the elegant, regional community-centered way of life. Living smaller is living better.

We're wising-up and replacing conspicuous quantity with simple and elegant quality.

We Are The Davids

Life is composed by higher Consciousness. The essence of that Light, no matter how dimmed or chaotic, is always there.

Loving Life enough to save it, heals us.

We are each the Davids slaying the darkness in the hearts of greed-addicted Goliaths.

Sometimes we are our own greedy, hyper-consuming, brand addicted, wasteful Goliath.

Love Loving a simply happy Life!

Love Life enough to *BE* higher Consciousness, so it outshines the darkness of greed and cruelty.

Tyrannical, power-hungry, often-pious personas have campaigned for the cultures of unconscious commerce that we now see collapsing into their own greed.

Aristocracies have done this through century after century of religious persecutions, holy wars, crusades, jihads, low consciousness media, contaminated education, divisive politics and judgemental religiosity. And while there are more of them now, the percentage that is the government and religion controlling priviledged class hasn't varied far off 1%.

They need to keep the 99% gossiping about personalities and party politics, rather than solutions to the problems.

As long as we're all obsessing about personalities rather than the energy misalignments causing the crisis, not much gets brought into The Light.

The chaos in the hearts of terrorists, and masses of their dumbed-down enablers, is the over-the-edge abyss.

We Davids slay Goliaths by *BE*ing the antidote to greed and cruelty.

Loving Life Is The Answer

When masses of us regain higher Consciousness and support local, green and conscious commerce, local communities of consciousness thrive and greedy Goliaths fall.

Love Loving Life enough to pay the price of shunning greedy enterprise and their toxic agendas. In the long run, you'll be saving everything.

Many great teachers have shown us Love is Life's answer. The great awakening of this era is the revelation that ALL Life on Earth is what we're here to cherish, celebrate and Love.

197

Must we only know what we've got, after
it's gone?

As consumers, let's stop bankrolling toxic
corporations and their politicizing agendas.

Let's have our state and local governments
support regional credit unions and banks. Let's
make our cities supportive of small business. Let's
lift communities up by changing the way wealth
flows away and up to the 1%.

Let's *BE* the kind of community we want to
live in.

Our Renaissance of Consciousness is an
awakening, a cleansing and a healing.

A Heart Call To The Wisdom of Women

Women in the U.S. work force outnumber men.
Women have virtually all the influence in the
marketplace. The women of North America make
almost 90% of the purchases. Women now have
THE industrial, corporate and social influence. It's
time for women to stop imitating the shark
behaviors of militarizing men and to bring the
higher Consciousness and wisdom of a Loving
nurturing mother into every social forum.

The economic collapses have created a
surprisingly wounded demographic group known
as "the beached white males". In an April of 2011
Newsweek cover story, U.S. social scientists
included college-educated, aged 35-64 white men,
among "socioeconomically disadvantaged
populations".

The greed-centered growth-at-any-cost agendas
of greed-addicted men have been turned upside
down. Men are humbled, confused, and at last
willing to regain Consciousness and Presence.

The shift is happening.

Life, business and politics aren't spectator sports. They're not about *being* on the winning team. They're about nurturing quality of Life.

This is the time for ALL mothers, grandmothers, women and conscious men around the world to shine the warmth and Light of Presence. This is the time to whole heartedly support conscious products, services, organizations, and agendas.

I recently attended a conference for conscious commerce, the Lifestyles of Health and Sustainability (LOHAS) forum in Boulder Colorado. This is a beautiful, warm and visionary community. My "Conscious Conversations" with some of the most inspiring LOHAS speakers are online at consciousworldsummit.com.

Communities of Consciousness are gathering near you.

To rejuvenate your hope and to feel included and inspired, gather with them.

If women do not bring the Light of Loving Life to every forum and endeavor, masses of us will feel the devastating loss of sanctuary—of *home*—that millions of us who've lost homes to greed are already enduring.

I do not wish this devastation on anyone.

I think of all the families who, throughout the history of marauding military crusaders, have lost their place to live. I feel the devastation of millions of people who've lost their homes, life savings, purpose, confidence, peace of mind, serenity of heart, health and well-being.

Those of us who've lost so much are called upon to teach, to co-create a better way of *BEing*.

This is your heart's call from Creation. Join me in co-creating communities and cultures that give peace its best chance.

It will have to get bad enough for masses of us to be shocked awake. The detonation of just one nuclear weapon, one dirty bomb, delivers us all to the powers of evil. Then perhaps the survivors will stand together to say, "Enough! No more! No more taxation to fund the bullying agendas of evil!"

Until then, your silence condones it.

We're all seriously at risk of losing quality of Life to the crusading agendas of big business addicted to getting bigger.

Every greedy war mongering government turns its corporate invasions into flag-waving holy missions sanctioned by their brand of Heaven.

Militarizing greed-addicts create hell not just with wars and terrorism; they do us all in with recklessly unconscious business.

The 80,000 devastated and homeless people of Fukushima, Japan know too well how a nuclear incident, in a time of Earth changes and climate crisis, can exterminate Life from the land.

For quality of Life to survive and to prevent more bereaved parents, and orphaned children from feeling the devastating loss of everything, *BE* the Presence of higher Consciousness throughout your days.

We each place huge pressures on electric companies to build nuclear and coal fired power plants to satisfy our wasteful demands. We're all responsible.

Be wise and conservative with the energy you use and the resources you consume.

Look deeply into the eyes and hearts of the children you Love and cherish. Feel your Love for the unborn children of your grandchildren—the generations that follow us.

You vote for rejuvenating quality of Life or for wholesaled chaos with every dollar you spend.

Two Minute Healing

From Despair to Possibility

To rise above the chaos that frays nerves, spirit and quality of life, *be* expansive gratitude for a beautiful presence that is in your life now.

Open your heart and mind and allow gratitude for what is good and beautiful to fill you.

When gratitude fills you, open the awareness through which you're experiencing this gratitude, and *BE* that peaceful light of warm, expansive Consciousness as long as you like.

Use this consciousness portal for yourself and for everyone who loves you.

Using this portal for a few minutes twice a day lifts you to a calm, resourceful, creative, higher plane. This goes far beyond merely quieting the mind through meditation. When you're opening and expanding your Consciousness, you're tuning up to higher frequencies of creativity and possibility, the higher dimensions of Creation.

The Harvard research, cited in chapter one, proves the benefits of this relaxation flow long after you've opened your mind to *be* higher Consciousness.

By being an open-minded, conscious, humble student of Now, you'll feel more flow, ease and synchronicity. You'll be tapping up to a higher realm of creativity.

To many old-school business people this seems like tree-hugger folly, but to Google it doesn't.

When they recruit new talent, they consider "Googliness"—the ability to solve problems in unique ways, inspire co-workers and thrive in a loose organizational structure.

They're looking for the creative joy that I describe as the Presence of higher Consciousness.

Genius flows from recognizing, feeling, being and then communicating the genus, the unique essential truth of a problem and its solution.

> Genius is simply communicating sustained, essential truth.

Every device and invention you use relies on the natural potentials of matter and our atmosphere. Science simply taps into what is already there.

The future's possibilities are right there, flowing all around you and through you now.

Our Community of Consciousness isn't snagged on the old follow-the-leader greed and power rules. They're our conscious economy's humble co-creators of Life's greatest possibilities.

Conscious commerce redefines how a successful life feels. Our transformation of business is blossoming a millennium of sustainable harmony. One person, one gathering, one community at a time, we're co-creating more conscious, beautiful, simple ways to *be*.

It's this Simple

Really, all we need to be doing is helping mothers and fathers co-create comfortable, harmless, safe and happy lives with their beloved children. That's IT!

After that, everything else falls in place.

Helping mothers and fathers co-create comfortable, no harm, safe and happy lives with their beloved children IS THE NEW ECONOMY!

It's that simple, and that's why economies are being rejuvenated by caring, conscious local heroes—the dolphins!

Old-school addicts balk at the possibility of living harmless lives. They argue that harmlessness, not only isn't possible, it isn't man's purpose!

That's the dominate and break-down Nature paradigm that brought us all to this brink of extremes.

Like the rest of Nature, we're intended to thrive through balance. Harmonious harmlessness IS the highest possibility of our purpose.

Evolution is cooperative Consciousness, the ongoing adaptation of organisms and environment. It's Life's becoming.

Considering the 13 billion year tenure of Nature's evolutionary process, human civilizations that grow and then collapse, are temporary and fallible.

Aristocracies that wanted to unplug the 99% from a responsibility for Nature's balance used religions to teach us God wants us to conquer the Earth. For the more educated they published and taught Darwinian beliefs that the evolution of species is essentially unpredictable happenstance and random mutation.

From this perspective, as British ethologist, and evolutionary biologist Richard Dawkins said, Nature is a "blind watchmaker".

This convinced generations of us to turn our backs on Nature and throw ourselves into industrialization's plans, as if quality of Life depended on that.

Then the system turned its back on Life.

A revolutionary, evolutionary viewpoint of higher Consciousness comes from the insights of French naturalist Jean-Baptiste Lamarck.

He lived during the French Revolution.

The Lamarckian worldview witnesses the world as a dynamic, symbiotic partnership with a "transformative alchemical force" adapting organisms up a ladder of complexity. He cited a second environmental force adapting Life through use and disuse of characteristics.

More modern research has proven him correct in seeing Life as the evolutionary becoming of "the alchemical and environmental force"; the Creation Consciousness that restores balance and harmony when an organism is out of alignment with its environment.

Rejuvenation isn't coming through power-addicted politics or the hypocritical old-school. It's blossoming through the offended sensibilities of the people marching and occupying, so we can all feel the brokenness of humanity's relationship with Life long enough for it to sink in and change our minds and hearts. They're inspiring action at every level of energy.

We can learn from the people's movements of Spain, Greece and the Arab Spring—they didn't stop at occupying the square. They moved to the neighborhoods, offering real solutions to immediate problems through local general assemblies and community groups. A sign left behind in one of the Spanish people's camps read, "We have not left—we have moved into your consciousness."

There is a great Cosmic plan orchestrating Life and our arrival at higher Consciousness—it's collapsing whole economies and ways of being and we're all a vital part of something really big.

The Zeitgeber

Is the collapse of institutions and economies, our great global shift and the awakening of higher Consciousness in accord with the seasons of the Cosmos?

In 1922 Alexander Chizevsky, a young Russian scientist, unveiled what was considered a preposterous theory: that the great social upheavals, unrest and revolutions coincided with the seasons of stormy weather on the Sun.

Suggesting that the tumultuous events leading to Russia's liberation from corrupt czarist rule was as cosmic as it was political threatened the newly ensconced Bolshevik Party and they sent him off to a gulag.

After sixteen years of imprisonment and rehabilitation, Alexander Chizevsky died in the mid-1960s.

He became a posthumous hero when the sheer breadth and foresight of his work was fully revealed. His painstaking records compared riots, revolutions and wars with sunspot activity for 2,000 years in 71 countries. More than 75% of the time, human unrest and revolutions occurred during a maximum period of solar storms. These are the geomagnetic events that create historically exceptional aurora borealis, like we're seeing in 2011-13.

The Cosmos operates according to a predictable timetable and science knows that it influences virtually every one of our biological processes. Every living thing has daily, weekly, monthly and even yearly rhythms.

The timekeeper of these rhythms is not built in, it's a Cosmic synchronizer, what German scientists began calling a zeitgeber.

It's considered an atmospheric synchronizer entraining the biological rhythms of all living systems.

In the 1970s the work of biologist Franz Halberg showed us its influence extends to the outer reaches of the Universe. [1]

Our relationship with the Sun sets the tempo of our planet's equilibrium, harmoniously guiding the interrelationships of all seasons and cycles. The Sun is the metronome of every living thing on Earth.

Solar cycles are approximately 11 years, during which sunspots build up and then our stormy Sun hurls gaseous explosions, solar flares, electrified bullet-like high-energy protons and magnetic fields with the force of billions of atomic bombs. This energy travels at 5 million miles per hour, disrupting electrical power, communication systems and the cellular processes of all living things—particularly the heart and the brain.

When the Sun is blowing off pent up energy, so are we. The stormy sun increases admissions to mental hospitals, traffic accidents and heart attacks and suicides—particularly among men.

It influences the stock market, our tendency to spend or save, acts of terrorism, and people taking to the streets to create social change.

The solar cycle of 2011 will continue to kick up in activity and reach its peak sometime in 2013. Experts predict increased mass excitement and social unrest.

According to 2011 research of the HeartMath Institute and Global Coherence Initiative, seasons of solar storms also give rise to human flourishing, with clear spurts in architecture, arts and science and positive social change. Old institutions are replaced with sustainable models. We find new ways of living.

There is no doubt that we're cosmically bonded with the Universe's dynamic process of becoming. We are part of a Big Bang Grand Plan that is influencing the decline of tyranny, the collapse of economies and a new renaissance.

What we're experiencing now is the great humbling—the Age of Aquarius shift from the dark ages of ego to our Renaissance of Consciousness.

Without the awe, you're in for the shock.

The Breaking Point

Usurious lenders are using arsenals of financial weaponry to weaken the 99%.

Indebted, enslaved, confused and afraid is how the old-school's aristocracy has been carefully taught to keep us in the follow the leader line.

In the home of the free and the brave, the old paradigm's military are turning weapons on peaceful citizens.

It's been a dark age for so long that many of the unconscious and brainwashed among us still can't see where the strict follow the leader line is leading us.

The Illuminati elite are suppressing health cures and energy solutions and engineering much of the social distress we're living. Their greed and power addictions are an enemy to their own wellbeing, and ALL of Life.

It's high time to apply higher Consciousness to industrial/military/financier trickery, and to help the greed-addicted and dark-hearted among us to see and be The Light.

We outnumber them by a million to one.

Beyond The Brink

This tipping point is humanity's turning point. Any neighborhood can be transformed, by one high Consciousness dolphin, into an intentional community of solidarity. We're seeing all kinds of possibilities collaborate online. I'm giving speeches for brilliant, Life-enhancing innovative communities that inspire us to rejuvenate the best and leave the rest.

In the picturesque mountain village of Nevada City, California the A.P.P.L.E. Center for Sustainable Living opened in 2009 as a regional center for developing skills, sharing knowledge and co-creating a sustainable community.

At a slightly higher elevation, Truckee, California opened "For Goodness Sake", to give people a lending library, shop and schoolhouse for uplifting the hopes, spirits and Consciousness of their region.

Put the name of your community and the words "sustainable", "green" or "consciousness" into an internet search engine and you'll see our new economy growing all around you.

You'll find people using this book, and others, with the films we reference and produce as community building tools. If you can't find a group, use meetup.com to create one!

We're each born with naturally flowing strengths, talents and gifts. These are your gifts to offer to Life, not to hide behind locked doors. *BE* your gifts!

Rejuvenation happens through higher Consciousness. There is nothing more powerful than an enlightened idea whose time has come.

People are starving for enlightened solutions.

Consciousness is the trademark of hope, innovation, leadership and prosperity. People connecting with grass-roots community consciousness, peacefully striving for harmlessness, will discover enthusiasm and support from some of the most unlikely places.

The Arab Spring and the evolving Occupy Movement are inspiring examples.

Inspiring teachers can't *be* Life for you. We each embody the higher Consciousness of Life's possibility for itself. *BE THE CHANGE* through the awareness you seek, the truth you find, the values you hold in your heart, the choices you make and the actions you take.

We've embarked on a new path, up to the high road, where higher Consciousness prospers and provides.

Regional Green Economies

The ratcheting-down of the white collar economy inspires innovative, heart-liberating new communities and regional business models.

A new-old kind of agricultural economy was clearly afoot when conferences for new farmers, like the one held in 2009 at The Stone Barns Center for Food and Agriculture in New York, had three times the expected attendance.

At "young farmers' mixers"—regional social events—in Vermont, attendance in 2009 tripled expectations. Educated young people are escaping cities and suburbs where they've been so carefully taught to fit in as cogs in the steely wheels of big industry. They're searching beyond their city limits to regional green industries.

And they're discovering a simply beautiful quality of Life.

The interests of many top students, even from Ivy League schools like Brown and Yale, are shifting from climbing teetering corporate ladders up to brass rings, to healing our Earth while finding honor and meaning in co-creating something valuable and real.

Rather than squeezing into rare jobs in shrinking, old-school companies, more graduates see the light of regional green economies and intellect-engaging hands-on relationship enterprises. These community-grown enterprises may harness renewable energy, use natural solutions for old problems or carefully grow the foods people eat.

Because of low consciousness big business food practices, we're sickened people who are both obese and malnourished.

Trends that make small organic farms a strengthening heartbeat of regional green economies include a widespread distrust of big food operations, a rising taste for local, organic produce, the dramatic growth of farmer's markets and the growing popularity of community-supported agriculture and business endeavors.

We're seeing a few county fairgrounds regaining their positions as fair and equal opportunity places for co-creating and celebrating the bountiful harvests of green fields and green enterprise.

Traditional fairgrounds have a unique and vital place within regional economies because they're community property, not owned and controlled by big business or government—hence the name *fairgrounds*.

Regional green economies are shifting.

Fairgrounds that struggled with urban relevancy, should be at the vanguard of growing regional green economies.

Inspired fair managers open their gates and doors to farmer's markets, business, barter, employment, education and networking events focused on energizing and celebrating regional excellence. This is exactly why fairgrounds were originally created. U.S. fairs celebrated their 200th birthday in 2011 and their season has come again.

This is one more example of how our economic and social shift moves what had become fringe, back into the quality-of-Life mainstream.

The Obamas' 2009 organic vegetable garden, planted on the lawn of The White House with school children, offered an inspiring example of letting go of ego and being hands-on, self-sustaining and more connected to Creation.

It's a new age—The Age of Consciousness!

New Crops of Consciousness

Across the continent small organic farms are inviting enthusiastic and participatory consumers to buy a share of their harvest for the year.

Most use the newest social media to keep their *families* interconnected.

The farms build community with optional events like "crop mobs". Their community contributes by making chores like weeding, picking beans or untangling drip irrigation lines, an event. Sometimes they get fed a big dinner before a dance-till-dawn party.

Parents see their children blossom from a day on the farm and a week's worth of work gets done in one happy afternoon.

The transformation of endangered family farms to community involved agriculture was delightfully documented in the film, *The Real Dirt on Farmer John* (Buena Vista, 2005).

This agricultural model of conscious commerce gives farms an assured, no-middle-man income stream. Their *families* have inclusion and the comfort of personally knowing where and who their weekly box of produce comes from.

Regional green innovations like this show us how many social activists shifted from just protesting—which is about stopping things—to championing brilliant solutions.

Protests really succeed when a visually unusual event focuses media attention on high consciousness solutions—what we're for.

Everything from renewable energy options to organics, and regionally produced fruit drinks and herb flavored oils are creating shared prosperity in farmers' markets and also on the shelves of conscious retailers like Whole Foods Markets.

Keep in mind that when you're eating fresh organic foods, your body gets the nutrition it needs from smaller servings. Organic farmers and their markets need to teach families how to eat well and affordably.

I lived in Austin, Texas when Whole Foods Markets was a funky counter-culture regional innovation. Now an international phenomenon, Whole Foods Markets still loves to stock their shelves with the harvests of regional ingenuity.

Canada's *Edible Cascadia* was the reinvention solution for a former network television reporter and realtor, Leigh Morrow. What started as hanging baskets of live herbs evolved to savory blends of healthy oils and vinegars. The consumer co-created concept grew into Edible Gardens, a major presence at regional farmer's markets throughout southern British Columbia, Canada.

They're now in Whole Foods Markets and they ship around the world through their web site.

"We'll always be a regional business with international possibilities", says entrepreneur Leigh Morrow. "We have an honest rapport with our customers and together, at the farmers' markets, we co-create our new ideas. Without my mother to mother relationships, this wouldn't have worked."

The conscious economy is the antithesis of mega-brand managers who occasionally emerge from corporate bunkers to observe total strangers in focus groups, while hiding behind one-way glass.

At my presentations, too many exhausted corporate managers have admitted that they work each day hoping to stay under the radar long enough to retire safely—and then hopefully to do something they can authentically love.

If that's your strategy find out if your retirement fund has already been raided to boost profits. It happens.

Conscious economies are founded on mothers and fathers trusting the Consciousness and integrity of who they're supporting.

We vote for or against Life, and humanity's future on Earth, with every dollar we spend. Honor harmlessness.

Product Stewardship

We'll always need conscious corporations. No region can grow and manufacture everything for itself, so it's worth learning about product stewardship programs.

They officially began in the 1980s by focusing organizational priorities on the Consciousness of design and performance. A review of management that implemented these practices is a list of recession surviving, industry-leaders. They're often the dolphins of new Conscious Commerce.

Consciousness Provides.

Product stewardship brings Consciousness to an organization's values and goals, and its infrastructure, tools and expertise. It manages energy efficiency, materials content, chemical emissions testing, design for recycling, packaging efficiency, and disposal plans.

Authentic product stewardship claims are genuine and not just spin-doctored hype or "greenwashing" that makes old-school agendas appear to be green.

Consciousness instills the management foresight to be your best before things get so bad that you're forced to wake up and reinvent as business is hitting bottom.

Our Bottoms

We all have two bottoms—one we sit on, the other we spiral down to. The second is a fall from the grace of higher Consciousness.

When something changes everything, we need to get off one, to avoid the other.

It has to get bad enough for people to regain consciousness, change, and heal their relationships. We all have our inner *bad enough* gauge.

How bad does it have to get—how deep and dark is your bottom before you enlighten the energies in your heart, regain Consciousness and decide to Love Loving Life and *be* the change?

The dolphins of our growing green economies aren't running away from inconvenient truths. Like heros, they're running to them, with higher social and environmental Consciousness.

They're students and teachers of Now.

Dolphins know that from Now the future is constantly being born. Every molecule of everything is now dancing with the Universe—Uni (one) verse(song).

Being is our invitation to arrive and dance with Creation's Consciousness.

All we'll ever have is Now—how lovingly we're dancing with it co-creates it.

The possibilities of Creation's Consciousness, are all around you, patiently waiting for you to stop the greedy gluttony, and to awaken and *BE* the dance.

Bliss is simply letting go of fear.

Innovations that rejuvenate quality of Life are born everywhere—including right there, where you are now.

California's Silicon Valley was regarded by many experts as the most creative place in the world.

That is shifting too. We'll see brilliant Life enhancing innovations from cooperative communities of higher Consciousness anywhere and everywhere.

Recently, after I'd given a live presentation on a cruise ship, a shark who'd been dragged to attend by a snapping turtle, closed in on me.

He snarled, "Your regional green enterprise is insignificant. We can't build a *great* economy on farmers' markets and green expos!"

I refrained from pointing out that's how the agricultural economy *was* created and, through exhibits at county fairs, that's how the industrial revolution caught on.

I went with, "Great isn't just big. It describes something exceptionally good. That's why Consciousness is growing so fast."

"Hmmmpf", he snorted while giving me the look he'd give to a cupcake before chomping it's sugary-frosted top off.

He turned on his tail and slipped into the darkness.

A comforting hand squeezed my arm. "Thank you, very much", his wife whispered. "I've never seen him approach *any* speaker before! He's a CEO, and you really made him think." She turned to crawl after him and chuckled, "He doesn't like to think!"

There is a lot of enlightenment still to be sparked and a lot of garage-inventor innovations still to be communally supported.

The traits of conscious management, products and services are listed in the following chapter.

Our conscious economy's renaissance is like a wildflower seed buried under concrete. It needs a raindrop to find it through a crack. Then, focused and determined to fully *be* alive, it will sprout to see the light of day.

Take heart,
hope's beginnings
have begun.

There are a lot of cracks in the concrete and
rainmakers are gathering at the greens.

CHAPTER 11

Our Renaissance of Consciousness

We've reached a brink—a tipping and turning point. We've all embarked upon the next great age. Our future will not mirror our past.

People who follow published roadmaps, hoping to find a place called *Business-as-usual,* will be lost.

Conscious people, less interested in roads and more conscious of the call of changing terrain, will follow higher Consciousness to communities of shared, simple solutions.

That community might be where you already are.

Something is changing everything. There is a new age dawning and our apocalypse brings a great rebirth of learning.

Here is the word "apocalypse" defined:

Apocalypse | əˈpäkəˌlips | noun

(Greek: "lifting of the veil") a term applied to the disclosure to certain persons of something hidden from the majority of humankind.

The word apocalypse is often abused to mean the end of life on Earth, possibly because those who want the masses confused, alienated and disturbed misinterpret the phrase *apokalupsis eschaton,* which literally means "revelation at the end of an æon or age."

For sharks addicted to the egoic old rules of money, power and control, the future will feel like the end.

As substance-abusers we can't clearly see that our own addictions are collapsing the quality of Consciousness in everything from relationships to families, communities and entire civilizations.

The key to recovery and prosperity is a Consciousness that's humble, gentle, open and willing to learn and grow from Now.

Consciousness is the radiance of BEingness.

Everything you can see is energy radiating through the air. Light energizes space to carry that energy to your eyes. However, if we were to compare light energies to musical scales, the human eye sees only one octave right in the middle. The Light of Creation's Consciousness is a vast spectrum, and new science is helping us see what we couldn't before.

The results of many classic scientific experiments now show a slightly different result than they did in the historic past. Scientists are witnessing our Universe evolving and opening up!

Devices that pull unlimited, clean, free energy from the atmosphere, like the ones seen in the film, "Thrive" (thrivemovement.com) , are poised to heal, transform and liberate Life on Earth.

We must not let the old world order's energy tyrants continue to keep free energy technology from us. Free energy births Our Renaissance of Consciousness.

When connected to what's really happening, higher Consciousness, reason, and logic will deliver solutions.

BEing higher Consciousness, we unite with the architecture of Creation and our next great age.

By *being* Life's solutions here on schoolhouse Earth, by *being* Love Loving Life, we ascend into higher energy dimensions.

Expanded Consciousness now lifts us from third dimensional limitations toward higher dimensions.

Life, this journey to the enlightenment of *being*, is the story of Creation's expanding Consciousness—and you co-create it.

In the final days of collapsing empires, those who survived to tell the story broke rank.

A Life Lived Lovingly

As you first awaken and open your eyes to a new day, what do you feel and then think? These moments reveal the intimate truth of your quality of BEing.

If each day is dreadful, you've dropped down into the depths of unconsciousness, the low-vibrational realms where chaos scrambles your days and nightmares fray your nights. Down there your mind latches onto painful thoughts and humiliating memories.

We all drop into lower Consciousness when external factors contaminate our internal presence. The debts of immediate gratifications, illusions of status and persona, the *trappings of success*, the doom agendas of terrorizing media, are all egoic energies of the money-driven parallel reality. We're all forgivably susceptible.

Taking time each day to *be* higher Consciousness lifts your vibration as it collapses the ego and expands the creative, problem-solving presence of peace.

This is what every loving teacher of spiritual enlightenment teaches.

Creation is Origin

Everything is the originality of Creation.

Creation is not repeating itself.

Creation is the dawn of each new day, the seasons repainting the landscapes, millions of interrelating evolving species, each moment of awareness, your fingerprints, your DNA, the iris of your eyes, and every aspect of your individual physical, mental and Consciousness Presence.

Nature is forever original and becoming.

BEingness is unfinished—reality and its constructs are unfinished.

Lynne McTaggart, is an award-winning journalist; she gathers and publishes important findings of the courageous scientists stepping outside the box to reveal the Oneness of the Consciousness field we're living in. (She inspired the character Katherine Solomon in Dan Brown's book, *The Lost Symbol*.)

Lynne describes Life and Space as being, "Like unset Jell-O. Even the largest molecules in the Universe, 'buckyballs,' are still unfinished."

Creation's Consciousness is actively becoming through you, as you.

We are Creation's children, descendants of Life dreaming Life.

Consciousness is Beyond Polarity

Consciousness is an energy realm not susceptible to polarity. Our Renaissance of Consciousness liberates us from constantly choosing sides—from getting pulled down into the fray by the polarizing leadership of fracturing systems.

Polarizing social systems are Life's brokenness.

Constantly choosing sides on a round planet is insanely unconscious.

By choosing sides on a spinning round planet, you take yourself out of Life's creative flow.

Competing and comparing block flow.

By choosing sides you've huddled with unconsciousness to inhale the rancid breath of those who are comparative, competitive, egoic and fearful. They've hardly evolved since the dark days of Rome's bloodthirsty Colosseum. Invaders make losers of those who choose sides.

Problems don't have sides! They simply have causes and solutions. When we're actively *BE*ing the solutions, we no longer energize the problems, or the pockets of their politically prospering proponents.

Our greatest truth is Oneness.

One person of Oneness can pull an entire community, country and planet together. Let oneness include you, too.

An adaptation can assure
the survival of a species.

Solutions will be relayed from community to community through the Internet.

Two Minute Healing

A Now Relationship
With Change

What would a perfect moment in time be
for you?

In your mind, create that sweet spot in time, the
most perfect moment you can imagine. Create
that ultimate moment, and then hold it as if you
can pause time. Let yourself *be* there for as long
as you'd like.

Be that moment now.

Notice the elements of that moment. What are
its ingredients? These are important aspects of
your Life that deserve prioritizing and nurturing.

Notice how the transcendence of fully *BE*ing
that moment changed you?

Also notice how long you were there before you
needed something to happen. Even when we
imagine perfection, change is necessary for it to
be alive. Change is Creation's *being*.

In The Age of Consciousness we will co-create
beautiful, sustainable, ways that lift Life up.

Your community's innovators, the tinkerers, and
their solutions for the highest good of ALL
deserve support and celebration.

When greatly inventive minds leave militarism to
regain Consciousness, peace will flourish. No
aristocracy can wage war without the participation
of mothers, fathers and their children. What

today's militaristic boot camps attempt to kill first is their recruits' Consciousness.

BE Creation Consciousness
through ALL that you do,
and ALL that you do
co-creates Creation.

Creative Chaos

Thoroughly cleaning a room in your home requires creative chaos while the housecleaning is happening.

As an artist moves back and forth from pallet to canvas, blending and mixing in stages to paint something beautiful, the less conscious eye sees chaos on both the canvas and on the pallet.

To create the statue of David, that slight youth who ended the tyranny of a giant, Michelangelo had to remove pieces of marble that didn't belong. It was only then that *the* David could share the light and exchange energies, and lessons of scale, with our admiring eyes. Do we grieve the marble pieces that were cut away or worry over what became of them?

No. We focus on the Creation, trusting that the cut-away pieces still exist—they, too, settled into various places within Life's art.

Every ending is a beginning.

We may fall into a low consciousness belief in chaos and the end of days if all we perceive is the chaos of Creation's housecleaning.

The worried, impulsive mind needing to see the finished end impatiently pulls us down out of Creation's flow. Those who perceive only endings will co-create their own.

The art of Creation Consciousness is to *be* the presence of the moment, peacefully where you are now, to open your Consciousness and co-create a gentle, simple Life of bliss.

Change and chaos
birth Creation.

Earth changes are shifting natural resources. While those addicted to old-school lifestyles of mega-money and status experience scarcities, communities of Creation Consciousness are blossoming.

When we have the epiphany that everything is worthy to be our trusted teacher, we become a delighted student, a witness and a wiser co-Creator. This is the sustainable bliss that co-creates sustainable lifestyles.

We all drop down into the depths of lower Consciousness at times; however now that we know the bliss of higher Consciousness, we'll resiliently bounce back.

Higher Consciousness is transformational.

As Earth changes happen, *beings* of higher Consciousness will have lifted themselves above the madding crowds to serenely live Our Renaissance of Consciousness.

Consciously, lovingly, patiently and optimistically navigate your *being's* course and you'll be amazed at how things that used to possess you can't injure you now.

Everything is attuned energy
becoming.

Two Minute Healing

BE The Renaissance of Consciousness

Use your presence and the powers of Now to co-create the future. Contribute to the mass Consciousness by co-creating the following: Imagine awakening, morning after blue-sky morning, to a peaceful, harmoniously conscious community. When a community's collective Consciousness is focused on quality of experience through quality of Consciousness, bliss is born with each new day.

Imagine how it will feel to *be* within a high Consciousness, enlightened and harmonious community, and to feel a peaceful oneness with ALL.

Be there. Feel how magnificent Life will *be*, how elegantly, lovingly, creatively simple and joyful your days—our days—are.

Fully imagine *being* there now and stay for as long as you desire.

Accept this future with your Consciousness and you are co-creating it.

Please *be* this beautiful probability for a few minutes whenever you think of humanity's future.

You are our future's co-creator.

Our migration to higher mass Consciousness will happen one person and one crisis at a time— because it has to get bad enough before we change our future's history.

Crisis is the nursery of competence.

All close-minded systems taken to extremes ultimately destroy themselves. Marauding addictions to greed and unreasonable power agendas collapse the redeeming qualities of all social and economic systems. Throughout human history greed and tyranny have collapsed communism, capitalism and socialism. And soon we will all be freed of the narrow-mindedness of an "ism".

Allow higher Consciousness to lead your way to sustainable balance. Let peaceful, innovative, Life Loving communities of higher Consciousness be your schools of higher learning.

Creation Consciousness is an architect, and with every moment, you are invited to be an open co-architect of possibility.

Seek Expansive, Loving Teachers

Enlightened teachers don't economize their enthusiasm. They're generous of spirit celebrators who invite your one-of-a-kind originality, talents, dreams and gifts to come out and play in the light, as the light.

Institutional functionaries, who try to control, box and convince you that they rent space on *the only* road to Heaven, are on a road that's closed.

Take a moment now to experience the blissful, Loving, creative freedom of Heaven to be vast, expansive higher dimensions of Creation's Consciousness. Open your mind, heart and *BE*ing to feel that now.

There are as many one-of-a-kind openings for arriving there as there are lives on Earth.

Creation doesn't, with each moment, energize originality for you to die from being the same.

There are as many paths and ways
to arrive at heavenly bliss
as there are BEings.

No matter how lost we may feel, expansive Consciousness opens us up to the heart of Creation.

Today's many great teachers of Consciousness are independently joyful individuals who invite us to open our minds and presence and to creatively Love Loving Life as it ALL is now.

ALL Life, this moment, is Creation's heartbeat.

Teachers of high Consciousness travel light and simply offer openings of enlightenment.

If they walked among us now, Buddha would not be a Buddhist, and Christ would not be a Christian. They were independent, individual teachers of Consciousness who simply, clearly invited us to witness and open the presence of Creation's Loving Oneness.

Unfortunately humans mystify the clarity and simple invitations of our greatest teachers by hoarding them inside complicating cultures and franchises.

Simply let there be enlightenment! It's out there in the sunshine, the moonlight and the invitations of a million twinkling stars.

The Dalai Lama is not the leader of a religion.

He describes the school and source of his personal faith with one word: kindness.

How simple. How very beautiful.

Imagine a whole world of kindness, and you'll be uplifted.

Begin by being kind to yourself. Love loving the original one-of-a-kind light of Life that is you.

Life Loving Life
blossoms bliss.

What if, as this moment now, you are fully and absolutely living up to your full potential?

What if everything throughout ALL of time brought you to this moment, these awakenings, and it's ALL been preparation?

What if it IS all good?

The truth is that everything throughout ALL of time did bring you to this moment, these awakenings, and it has ALL been preparation for the arrival of Now!

Just Love Loving Life as it ALL is Now!

Let go of competing, comparing and judging Creation. Open your heart and mind to accept everything simply as it is now. Surrender the inner war that you've been so carefully taught to wage.

Every moment you've ever had with every soul you've ever loved is energy co-creating the presence of Now. Open up to feel that. Forgive Life and Creation for everything and let your spirit soar!

Let lightness bathe and cleanse away toxic tightness in and around your heart and mind. Allow peace to lift conflict off your mind and heart. Let go and open to Love Loving Life!

Creation
Loves Love,
is grateful for gratitude
and is
being everything
Now.

Skills For The Dolphin Within

- Each day collapse your ego by *being* higher Consciousness.

- *Be* a humble, enthusiastic student of Now.

- *Be* higher Consciousness and generous of spirit.

- Have a heart open to hope and possibility and a mind open to the reason and logic of Now.

- Ask courageous questions that invite honesty and improvement.

- Honor ALL of Life. We're in this together.

- Create your own University of Now and be generous with wisdom.

- ✦ It is never crowded on the extra mile, so get outside the box and go the extra mile. On that journey *be* a student of the changing terrain.

- ✦ Experience where Consciousness, energy, trends, solutions and possibilities are flourishing. Complement these with your communal talents, passions and hopes.

- ✦ Befriend people who are living your dream. Find experienced, generous-of-spirit mentors.

The power of any answer is embedded in the courage of the question.

Ask profound questions that invite relearning.

Traits of Conscious Products

A conscious product experience has people thinking, "Gee, they thought of everything."

That creates the buzz among the people who, at the market and dining tables ask, "Have you tried___yet?"

Dolphin managers gather people who generate a buzz. If you're not feeling that buzz of excitement and energy in your organization, who is going to feel it in the marketplace?

If you're not energized and excited by what you're co-creating, why should anybody else be?

Conscious products have:

+ Research, design and development that is highly aware of evolving ease of use, practicality, efficiency, durability and affordability.

+ The elimination of engineered obsolescence and the reinforcement of product durability.

+ Flexibility with consumer customization in mind, and upgradeable features to extend hardware life.

+ Design for reuse, recyclability and safe disposal at the end of product life.

+ Use of recycled materials when justifiable.

+ Improvement of energy efficiency every step of the way.

+ Consumer education about your product's higher Consciousness, its justifiable value price point and how they may easily and most consciously use it.

Traits of Conscious Service

+ A permeating presence that says we're human, we're conscious, we're with you, we get it—and we've tried to think of everything!

+ Compassionate customer service capable of appropriate individualization.

+ A rapport with creating ongoing improvements.

+ Valued, trained and motivated employees who realize providing the excellence of higher Consciousness for others is honorable and worthy of the highest respect.

+ A centered awareness that we're all in this together.

Traits of Conscious Management and Politics

Consciousness: INSPIRES people to awareness, agendas, and actions that lift Consciousness and inspire us to be better and do better.

Consciousness: Is a humble student LEARNING from the grassroots values of loving mothers and fathers.

Consciousness: LISTENS to people and monitors social media because truth, trends and shifts in the winds of change are first published there.

Consciousness: Is adaptive CREATIVITY flowing as communal benefits.

Consciousness: Is COURAGE giving emerging truth, no matter how inconvenient it may be, room to expand into awareness and precise action.

Consciousness: RECOGNIZES the sources of forces as either a Love of Life or an addiction to power. Groups that suppress free speech and truth by calling it treasonous are a red flag for dictatorship, not democracy.

Consciousness: INVESTIGATES the facts and clearly communicates the truth and powers of Now.

Consciousness: FACILITATES fact-based truth and informed discussions.

Consciousness: Is CHARACTER consistently sustaining what is for the greatest long-term good of all. A person of character does not endorse placing even one mother's child in harm's way for the empowerment of a conqueror's greed.

Consciousness: Is a HUMBLE and wise diplomat, eliciting enlightened, cooperative actions.

Consciousness: Exemplifies COURAGE even when it erodes popularity among the unconscious, greedy and deadly. Courage isn't swagger, posturing, or bravado. It's born of humility. Courage is having the humble wisdom to listen, learn and to experience ALL perspectives before co-creating the win/win/win.

Consciousness: Is PEACEFUL and does not attack or defend, but rather gently leads people to the truth and to enlightened reasoning.

Consciousness: Is COMPASSION for ALL, far beyond just the people wearing our team's colors.

Consciousness: COMPENSATES based on effective performance.

Consciousness: Has the engaging and honest CHARISMA that inspires enlightened goodness in others. People follow Consciousness and the leadership that inspires trust and enlightened actions.

Consciousness: Embodies COMMON SENSE, the ability to create a logical and rational understanding of the real reason things are happening. Calls to action are backed up logic and reason that people sense is for the highest good.

Consciousness: Is CENTERED, calm, and resourceful.

The Wish

This book's ending marks its beginning. The dawning of the fresh new days of Our Community of Consciousness.

It's an invitation to the high road and higher grounds of higher Consciousness. It's a call to rise above the crowds, to be transcendently aware that the road humanity has been traveling is at a fork. One option is to march to the same dollar-addicted drummers. That path leads down to doom. The other leads up to Life's highest possibilities. It calls out for courage because at some levels the path disappears and we must instinctively follow our heart's lead.

Others of pure heart will welcome you when you arrive.

The greatness of any country, society, economy or system isn't in its bigness or its might. It's in the hearts of its people and the health of the land below them, the skies above them, and the pure, clean waters that are Life's bloodstream here on schoolhouse Earth.

This book sounds many notes and is composed on many levels. As your Consciousness opens, and your presence expands and enlightens, you'll feel its music, the Universe's song and the poetry of Oneness at new levels.

If you've made it this far with this book's journey, you are Life's hope for itself.

Let us begin to end with a wish.

My life has been lifted to heights of Love, peace, transcendence, presence and abiding, expansive happiness through *being* higher Consciousness.

My Life's journey is wishing this for you.

I am so grateful for the courage of your ego's surrender, and the hope and Consciousness that brought us to this wish.

I feel you, and our Oneness, as I write these words and as you read them now.

I am *being* gratitude and expansive hope with you, for you, and for ALL of Life.

BE the bliss of higher
Consciousness.
Love Loving Life
and
BE well within.

ConsciousWorldSummit.com

Our online, ongoing summit is as fresh and hopeful as tomorrow's potentials.

Imagine a Mind Spa offering you healing, enlightening, consciousness expanding sweet spots in time—moments that open you up to *be* higher Consciousness.

Imagine accessing an online course giving you new insights, articles and short films that are leapfrogging solutions around our world.

Imagine connecting with our Community of Consciousness as we share ways to rejuvenate communities, conscious commerce and careers.

Imagine this global gathering available in 52 languages.

Now you're connecting with what this book begins.

We're fulfilling the hope of every Loving mother around the world—that her family and community may be allowed to peacefully, simply and joyfully Love Loving Life.

Join Peter and Our Community of Consciousness today @ ConsciousWorldSummit.com

End Notes

Chapter 1

1. *Light After Life: Experiments and Ideas on After-Death Changes of Kirlian Pictures*, 1998, NY, Backbone Publishing Co.

2. *The Journal Of Alternative And Complementary Medicine*, 1999; 5 (4): 383-9.

3. *American Journal of Chinese Medicine*, 2003; 31(4): 623-8

4. *American Journal of Chinese Medicine*, 2001; 29(1): 17-22

5. Acup Electro-Ther Res Intl J, 1992; 17: 7 5 - 9 4

6. Measurement and analysis of the infrasonic waves from the emitted qi. Proceedings of the First World Conference for Academic Exchange of Medical Qigong. Beijing College of Traditional Chinese Medicine, 1988.

7. *Neuro Report*, 2000; 11: 1581-5

8. *Stroke*, 2000; 31(3): 568-73

9. *Psychosom Med*, 1987; 49: 493-507

10. Int J Neurosci, 1982; 16(1): 53-8

11. *Psychoneuroendocrinology,*1997; 22 (4): 277-95

12. J Pers Soc Psychol, 1989; 57 (6): 9 5 0 - 6 4

13. J Clin Psychol, 1989; 45: 957-74

14. *Alcohol Treat Quart*, 1994; 11: 13-87

15. J Clin Psychol,*Health, Quality of Life Outcomes*, 2003;1(1): 1 0

16. *Education*, 1986; 107: 49-54

Chapter 2

1. Source: "Icons of the Field" conference DVD WDDTY Ltd. 2006

2. *Time* (March 19, 1979, p. 86)

3. *Remote Viewers: The Secret History of America's Psychic Spies* by Jim Schnabel p 171+

4. "Icons of the Field" conference DVD WDDTY Ltd. 2006

5. *Materials Research Innovations*, 1999; 3 4 9–5 9

6. *Ziran Zazhi*, (Nature Journal) [Chinese] 1988; 11: 567–71

7. *Frontier Science: Living the Field*, 2007: 22

8. www.alivewater.net/research/ludwig.htm

9. *Frontier Science: Living the Field*, 2007: 21-22

10. Steven Rose & Robyn Williams, 2002. Interview with Steven Rose on The Science Show, ABC Radio National.

11. *What Is Intelligence?: Beyond the Flynn Effect* Cambridge, UK ; New York:Cambridge University Press, 2007.

12. McTaggart, L.,The Field , N.Y. Harper 112-19 2008

13. McCraty, R. et al. *The Electricity of Touch: Detection and Measurement of Cardiac Energy Exchange Between People*, in Pribram KH, ed. Brain and *Values: Is a Biological Science of Values Possible?* Mahwah, NJ: Lawrence Erlbaum Associates, 1998: 3 5 9 – 7 8

14. http://www.physorg.com/news/ 2011-04-demystifying-meditation-brain-imaging

15. *Psychiatry Research*, 2011; 191: 1 36-43

Chapter 3

1. R.D. Nelson et al, Journ of Scientific Exploration, 1998; 12(3): 425-54

2. Tiller, W.A. 'What are Subtle Energies' *Journal of Scientific Exploration*, 1993; 7(3):293-304

3. Hagel J.S., *Social Indicators Research*, 1994;47:153-201

4. McTaggart, L.,The Field, N.Y. Harper 212, 2008

5. Sci Res Maharishi Transc Med TM-Sidhi Prog Coll Papers, 1989; 4: 2566-82

Chapter 4

1. "Icons of the Field" conference DVD WDDTY Ltd. 2006

2. Klein, N., *The Shock Doctrine: The Rise of Disaster Capitalism*, Picador Publishing 2008

Chapter 5

1. "Icons of the Field" conference DVD WDDTY Ltd. 2006

Chapter 7

1. www.ajc.com/news/nation-world/science-panel-get-ready-1231701.html

Chapter 8

1. MD Lambert, *The Cathars*, Blackwell Publishing, 2004, pg. 15

Chapter 10

1. Lynne McTaggart, *The Bond*, Hay House, 2011, pg. 45

End Notes

INDEX

About The Author

Peter McGugan is the founder of Conscious World Summit—an online ongoing gathering place for the Community of Consciousness.

He is a best selling-author, top-rated speaker, broadcaster and transformational teacher.

California's association executives rated him their speaker of the year and meeting planners have rated him among North America's top speakers.

This book follows Beating Burnout which became an instant best-seller that was distributed internationally.

Peter's second book, *When Something Changes Everything: Recovering from Change and Loss*, is a reinvention and recovery classic.

Peter is ushering in our new paradigm with films, speeches, retreats, book clubs, consulting and his live one-man theatrical productions.

Each month you can experience new films, interviews and healing audio programs at ConsciousWorldSummit.com.

Visit

C o n s c i o u s W o r l d S u m m i t . c o m

uplifting films
healing audio programs
inspiring articles
conscious communities
events

CPSIA information can be obtained at www.ICGtesting.com
Printed in the USA
LVOW091024220512

282770LV00001B/9/P